Emotional Literacy in the Early Years

Christine Bruce

Los Angeles | London | New Delhi
Singapore | Washington DC

First published 2010

SAGE Publications Ltd
1 Oliver's Yard
55 City Road
London EC1Y 1SP

SAGE Publications Inc.
2455 Teller Road
Thousand Oaks, California 91320

SAGE Publications India Pvt Ltd
B 1/I 1 Mohan Cooperative Industrial Area
Mathura Road
New Delhi 110 044

SAGE Publications Asia-Pacific Pte Ltd
33 Pekin Street #02-01
Far East Square
Singapore 048763

Library of Congress Control Number: 2010922464

British Library Cataloguing in Publication data

A catalogue record for this book is available from the British Library

ISBN 978-1-84920-602-0
ISBN 978-1-84920-603-7 (pbk)

Typeset by C&M Digitals (P) Ltd, Chennai, India
Printed by CPI Antony Rowe, Chippenham, Wiltshire
Printed on paper from sustainable resources

For Dad, who gave me my energy and determination

Contents

Acknowledgements ix
About the Author x
About this Book xi
Electronic Resources xii

1 Why Emotional Literacy is Good for Your School **1**
An Introduction to Emotional Literacy 1
The Context 2
Where to Start with Emotional Literacy 3
The Importance of Establishing a Common Understanding 5
The Potential of Emotional Literacy 6
The Problems with Emotional Literacy 7
The Significance of Emotional Literacy to Education 7
The Action Research Context 9
Further Reading 13
Electronic Resources 14

2 Emotional Literacy as an Approach to Learning and Teaching **15**
How Small Changes Can Have a Big Impact 16
Developing and Using Space 17
Planning for Emotional Literacy 20
Organising Teaching 24
Keeping a Reflective Journal 26
Further Reading 27
Electronic Resources 28

3 How an Emotionally Literate Approach can Support Inclusion **29**
Creating an Oasis for Children with Social, Emotional and Behavioural Needs 31
A Different way to Form Groups 35
Puppets and their Uses 38
Building Self Esteem 43
Further Reading 45
Electronic Resources 45

4 Using Emotional Literacy Across the Curriculum **46**
Classroom Initiatives 46
Circle Time as an Approach 46
Communication Skills 47
Story and Drama 49
Using Photography 52
Extension Activities 55

Parachute Activities 63
Outdoor Play 65
Further Reading 66
Electronic Resources 66

5 The Role of the Adult 67
General Points 67
The Role of Parents 68
Overcoming Barriers 68
What is Partnership? 70
Homework 70
Parents Meetings 71
The Role of Support Staff 72
Involving Parents and Families 73
The Role of the Teacher 74
The Importance of Teacher Self Esteem 76
Attachment 77
Working as a Collaborative Team 77
The Whole School Approach 78
Further Reading 80

6 Implications for Practice 81
Collected Data 82
Discussion of Research Effectiveness 87
The Advantage of Reflection 89
The Responsibilities of the Teacher (Communication) 91
The Impact on Pupils and the School Community 92
Implications for Professional Practice 92
The Emotionally Literate School Community 93
Final Word 93
Further Reading 94
Electronic Resources 94

References 95

Index 101

Acknowledgements

There are many people whom I should like to thank for their support, participation and patience: my colleagues Janice Mackenzie, Catherine Douglas, Kerry Mackie, Ann Macleod and Andrea Stark for their enthusiasm and support at various points along the journey; the children and parents of Parkhead Primary School who became involved in the project; and those who in addition allowed their photographs to be used in this book. To Corrine Mackenzie, Shamim Aslam and Anna Martin thanks for your support in the nursery, and Christine Robertson for yours in primary 1. I would also like to thank Catherine-Mary Thomas, Dorothy Johnstone and particularly Liz Lockhart who not only provided a listening ear, but additionally gave her time to proofread this book.

The original project would not have been possible without the support and confidence of our headteacher at that time, Carol Gordon, and then acting head, Rita Angus. Nor would I have reached this point without the encouragement and advice of Gillian Robinson of the University of Edinburgh, and more recently the editorial guidance of Jude Bowen, Amy Jarrold and the editorial team at SAGE Publications.

My quest to discover Emotional Literacy in action brought me into contact with a variety of colleagues exploring similar themes and to them I give my thanks for their support and advice, particularly Susan Maclennan, for showing me around her school and sharing her practice.

My family deserves very special thanks since they often came second to project work: my sons David and Peter, and especially my husband Malcolm for his encouragement, patience and understanding – for keeping me sane!

About the Author

Christine Bruce has an energetic personality and great love of the outdoors. With almost 30 years' teaching experience she would describe herself as simply an ordinary class teacher who takes pride in her work. She continually strives to improve her teaching and became one of Scotland's first chartered teachers by completing a postgraduate Masters degree in teaching at the University of Edinburgh in 2006 and by meeting the enhanced standard for teaching that a chartered teacher must demonstrate.

Christine has long held the view that education should be child-centred and believes unequivocally that children achieve most when they are happy and comfortable in their environment. She feels that developing a holistic Emotionally Literate approach is the answer to many of her concerns. She sees a teacher's role as more than a simple educator – working with parents, leading after school clubs and outdoor activities throughout her teaching career.

As a newly qualified chartered teacher she presented her final research project at the inaugural conference of Chartered Teachers. Her work won an award at the BERA research conference in 2007 and she has since presented at the SERA 2009 national conference. She led the West Lothian Network for Health and Wellbeing for two years before accepting a secondment as a teaching fellow to Moray House School of Education at the University of Edinburgh. She is currently working within the infant years department of a large semi-rural primary school. Christine feels her experiences have broadened her views and strengthened her teaching. She continues to be interested in action research and like all dedicated teachers manages a full and active working week. She believes in the importance of Emotional Literacy as a life skill in our modern world.

About this Book

I hope that through presenting my experience of undertaking this action research project in an honest and realistic manner that it will in some way, be it whole school, class, group or indeed at an individual level, encourage you to have a go and take on a similar project. I have learned such a lot from the experience, about myself, my teaching approach and working with my colleagues. I expect most readers will dip into this book for a variety of purposes and so the structure is intended to facilitate this approach with each of the six chapters able to stand alone.

Each chapter includes questions to support reflection, and ends with some suggestions for further reading. The resources were made to suit the specific needs of our children and are available on the website www.sagepub.co.uk/christinebruce for you to adapt to suit your particular needs.

Readers will notice that although the work is related to education across the UK it retains something of a Scottish flavour which soundly demonstrates the close links behind our common educational values. This underlies the principles of Emotional Literacy as an approach to bring the people of the world closer together through a common understanding and empathy, a greater sense of resilience and wellbeing. Readers are encouraged to read over and around the specific curricular references and reflect on how the ideas could be extracted and used or adapted to suit their own situation and individual needs.

Throughout this book, I have made use of the voices of children and parents recorded in my journal observations. These are used to give greater depth and richness to points being made and to help the work become more alive, within the context of a working classroom. In addition, I would be interested in any feedback and ideas that have worked for you.

Ethical Considerations

To give credence to this action research project (or indeed to the one you may undertake) I have taken particular time and attention in the planning, preparation and piloting of suitable research vehicles and to rigorous, systematic data collection. Confidentiality has been maintained at all times. Through working in collaboration with the nursery nurses and support assistants, I have used investigator triangulation, which minimises the opportunity for researcher bias on the data. I also kept parents informed of our work through an initial information letter, progress newsletters, open evening/afternoons and daily news bulletins at the nursery front entrance. The parents, children and staff were all informed of the research findings and invited to read my dissertation prior to submission. All pupil guardians gave permission for the use of photography.

Electronic Resources

Electronic resources for this book can be found at: www.sagepub.co.uk/christine bruce for use in your setting. For a full list please see below.

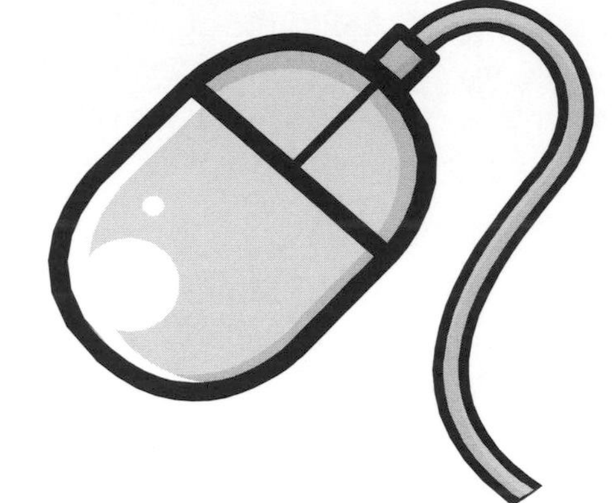

Chapter 1

1.1 Project Aims and Objectives
1.2 Project Action Plan
1.3 Project Timetable
1.4 Revised Timetable
1.5 Nursery Pupil Interview
1.6 Primary Pupil Interview
1.7 Nursery Parent Interview
1.8 Primary Parent Interview
1.9 Emotional Expression Drawings

Chapter 2

2.1 List of Stories for Encouraging Discussion
2.2 Transition Sheet: About Me
2.3 Example of Emotional Literacy Class Contract
2.4 'How I Feel' Worksheet

Chapter 3

3.1 A Checklist for Emotional Inclusion
3.2 Individualised Train Timetable Template
3.3 Positive Behaviour Support Cards
3.4 Puppet Letter

Chapter 4

4.1 Circle Time Lesson
4.2 Small World Play
4.3 Wanted Poster and Resource Sheets
4.4 Parachute Games
4.5 Ideas for 'A Pocket of Instant Fun'
4.6 Ideas to Establish Creative Outdoor Fun
4.7 Games Instructions

Chapter 6

6.1 Useful Web Addresses

Why Emotional Literacy is Good for Your School

In this chapter, I consider:

- **What is Emotional Literacy?**
- **Why is it important?**
- **What benefits can it bring to a school or setting?**

An Introduction to Emotional Literacy

Have you considered the ethos you are aiming for? If the answer is that you want to achieve an enthusiastic and supportive learning community where there is a sense of belonging, where each pupil is valued for their unique contribution, where children have built the confidence, independence and resilience to enjoy challenge, explore creativity and fully engage in rich and deep learning experiences, where children respect each other and have a sense of pride in their achievements, then you could start with considering **Emotional Literacy**.

To Think About:

- *What sort of classroom ethos are you trying to achieve?*
- *What sort of class do you want to have?*

What is Emotional Literacy?

Emotional Literacy is a way of 'being' not just of 'doing'. It is a pedagogical approach concerning teaching style and learning environment which you can develop with your pupils as a community approach to inclusion. Salovey & Mayer (1990) originally defined it as a type of 'social intelligence' which enables people to differentiate between emotions and the resulting actions. The teacher's role is then to provide a safe but rich and challenging learning environment where children are free to grow socially and emotionally, while academically nurtured. Mia Kellmer Pringle (1986) used Maslow's well known hierarchy of needs pyramid to develop a simplified theory for the needs of children. Basically, only when a child feels emotionally safe and secure in their environment will they undertake the challenge and risk needed to learn. New learning challenges our self confidence; we need resilience to overcome disappointment or acknowledge our mistakes. Many children are simply not ready to do that and need our support to explore challenge safe from ridicule. Successful deep learning can only take place where recognition and praise is given not only for what is correct but for effort and for solutions found through collaboration. This type of supporting yet challenging environment, where collaboration is encouraged with 'scaffolding' to support and extend learning, follows the principles of social constructivism, allowing children to blossom into independent learners through developing self esteem, self control and social skills.

The Context

This book is based in particular on the Emotional Literacy project which I undertook as a nursery class teacher, working at that time towards a postgraduate degree in education. The project followed and documented an extended action research initiative initially with 76 nursery children aged between 3 and 5 years, then subsequently followed 19 of those children aged between 4½ and 5½ years through the transition into their first school year, with myself as their class teacher. Those 19 children were then joined by six other children who had all attended a neighbouring nursery. The six additional children had not had an explicit focus on Emotional Literacy, which allowed for a contrast of data.

In the very beginning during the school annual audit, the staff expressed a concern that there seemed to be a steady decline in the general levels of respect and discipline around the school. It was felt that our attainment targets were affected through poor attitudes being displayed by a growing number of pupils towards the school community, and particularly by many of the older children. This lack of social skills was perceived by the staff as a particular concern despite the existing good use of circle time, positive discipline and reward strategies throughout the school. The feeling was highlighted further in a whole school pre-project baseline survey in which data were collected from children, parents and in-school adults regarding perceptions of in-class and out-of-class behaviours. The result was a whole-school commitment to introduce and develop a programme of Emotional Literacy.

It was hoped that focusing on Emotional Literacy would establish an inclusive feeling of responsibility and belonging between pupils and the school community. Further it was hoped that the issues raised in the audit would be addressed through this initiative while not just maintaining but improving attainment. However, to successfully achieve any pedagogical change, staff need to believe in the worth of an initiative and understand the principles behind it (Fullan, 1991). This requires training; in our case an initial whole-staff training session was followed by professional reading around the subject and then the trial of resources led by a small group of committed staff. Effectively the whole school began to participate in the action research process, which as Cohen, Manion & Morrison (2000: 226) assert is *'a powerful tool for change and improvement'.*

Introducing Emotional Literacy from the earliest stages in the nursery class played a foundational part in the wider whole-school plan. To make progress required not only staff collaboration within the nursery setting but also with the whole-school working group, and dialogue with other professionals, the management team, and vitally, with our parents. The focus within the nursery was supported at that time by the 3–5 curriculum, SCCC (1999), which was first and foremost based on promoting social skills. Writing as an experienced teacher it was my contention that these skills were the foundation of all education, a view which is readily supported in current educational literature and in the new curricula across the United Kingdom.

Where to Start with Emotional Literacy

In the beginning of your project it will be prudent to ensure that all staff involved have a clear and shared perception of your goal. It would also be prudent to have a little background knowledge and a common understanding of what Emotional Literacy is. It is important then to consider how the concept has evolved and the many benefits the approach can bring.

Why Emotional Literacy?

Emotional Literacy (EL) is still a relatively new and growing area in education and is based on the theory of Emotional Intelligence (sometimes referred to as EI or EQ); the ability to process emotional information. This theory is usually considered to have been developed by Salovey & Mayer in 1990, the term 'Emotional Intelligence' making the simple link between the affective and the cognitive domains. Today their work is supported through contemporary research (Smith, 2004; Blakemore & Frith, 2005) which tells us that the brain plays a central role in emotional response. We know, for example, that the pre-frontal cortex is involved in social, cognitive and emotional processes such as the regulation of attention, pain, self control, flexibility and self awareness and seems very sensitive to the environment. We also know that our brain makes strong and crucial connections between our senses and our emotions (Damasio, 2003).

Emotional Intelligence is often referred to as Emotional Literacy in educational circles, the term 'Literacy' suggesting a practical process or concept which one can be taught 'to read'. I believe there is an innate element to emotion which through careful nurturing can be developed and refined, and then further skills taught developing into what may be known as Emotional Literacy.

The initial research of Salovey and Mayer has been reframed and internationally popularised during the last 10 years through the works of Daniel Goleman (1996, 1998). Goleman made the case that emotional and social intelligence is more relevant than conventional intelligence in the workplace and for a successful life. Salovey and Mayer saw Emotional Intelligence as being made up of four distinct

• Self awareness	the capacity to recognise your feelings as they happen
• Emotional control	the resilience to self manage your emotional reactions
• Self-motivation	perseverance and determination to work with your emotions to overcome challenge
• Empathy	emotional sensitivity to other people's feelings
• Handling relationships	self confidence and social skills to work collaboratively or to lead people.

Figure 1.1 Bringing the key areas of emotional intelligence together

branches; put very simply these are perception, thought, understanding and management. These could be seen as foundational to the five domains for Emotional Literacy laid out by Goleman (1996). The DCSF *Seal Strategy* (2005) is based on a similar set of five core aspects: self awareness, managing feelings, empathy, motivation, and social skills, which are considered basic to the development of Emotional Literacy. These key areas are brought together in Figure 1.1.

The work of Howard Gardner (1983) on multiple intelligences could be considered to take a parallel view and has had a significant impact on teaching and learning. His theory stresses the breadth of intelligences including interpersonal and intra-personal intelligence which both relate to Emotional Literacy. Interpersonal intelligence relates to taking account of other people and their emotional states and intra-personal intelligence, recognising and managing our own emotions successfully. The idea of Emotional Literacy is therefore nothing new but it demonstrates a growing awareness of the multi-faceted nature of intelligence and the importance of understanding the relevance of this as an approach to learning and teaching.

To Think About:

- *Who should provide this nurturing?*
- *Is this within the remit of teachers?*

Governing bodies recognise the potential implications of disruptive or indeed compliant behaviour masking underlying emotional problems which teachers often feel ill qualified to handle. There is also support in Christie et al. (1999) for the assertion that many children demonstrate a lack of empathy which challenges teacher professionalism. However, successful teachers can and do encourage the development of intra-personal awareness and self esteem. If there is even some small cognitive element to emotion, then, as Sharp (2001) acknowledges, the skills of control and understanding should be nurtured, taught and practised in the form of Emotional Literacy. To be really effective these skills need to be modelled and taught not only by individual teachers but as a whole-school community, including both teaching and non-teaching staff. Weare (2007) believes there is unequivocal evidence to support a whole-school approach to Emotional Literacy.

Figure 1.2 Continuum of Emotional Literacy

The Importance of Establishing a Common Understanding

From the outset I strongly suggest that if you are considering undertaking a project to develop Emotional Literacy then you should create your own shared definition or understanding, through teasing out and exploring existing definitions to consider which aspects you agree with. The key to Emotional Literacy is, as Mathews et al. (2002: 3) establish, the ability not only to recognise emotions in oneself and in others but to have some understanding and even control of these emotions, to *'assimilate them in thought'*. Achieving Emotional Literacy could be considered to be a continuum where initially one must first learn to recognise basic emotions through facial expression and body language, then develop an understanding of what that means before one can handle and express emotions appropriately (see Figure 1.2). The nursery project started through developing an initial recognition which naturally followed along the continuum through simple understanding and appropriate handling and expression of emotion, to active understanding and expression of empathy, a skill that many adults are still rehearsing. It is, after all, possible to recognise emotion but fail in the capacity of empathetic understanding, instead showing apathy and indifference.

This crucial ability to understand and appropriately express emotion must also depend on socio cultural factors, in keeping with the ecological perspective of the Bronfenbrenner model (1979). This model emphasises the important influence of the wider environment centred around the child's 'microsystems', or micro–environment, in a nested effect. These uniquely influence individual development and behaviour, through an ever widening and complex mix of environmental and social contexts and experiences. The effect of different personal experiences changes the way we perceive and express emotion, both in ourselves and others. To take account of this, any definition formed should acknowledge people's differing abilities to understand that other people 'feel' different things, even from a shared experience. Goleman (1998) suggests this shared understanding or empathy may require maturity to develop, however I believe it could be initiated in the early years. Support exists for this in the work of Brown & Dunn (1996), who found that young children of 3–4 years could express their understanding of emotion in others.

An essential consideration in forming your own definition is therefore the different individual interpretations each of the staff has developed in relation to past experience. For this project it was important that this awareness of individual and personal difference in understanding was acknowledged and as far as we were able, and a common understanding of Emotional Literacy developed, allowing construct validity or a shared, clear and common focus with which to gauge observations in the same light. To this end the staff immediately involved in the project each wrote their personal understanding of Emotional Literacy. After reflection together, with discussion on our personal understandings and reading, the following definition was agreed as our common understanding at that time and shared with our nursery parents. It includes our recognition of differences both amongst ourselves and our pupils and appreciates the need to accept children as they are, because of their different life experiences. I believe this individual level of acceptance is fundamental to Emotional Literacy.

> Emotional Literacy is a developed awareness and understanding of one's own and others' emotions. This information guides our thinking and is expressed in our communication and behaviour. Further, it is the understanding that individuals feel emotions in different ways and therefore have different responses depending on their life experience. (Parkhead Nursery Staff, 2004)

The Potential of Emotional Literacy

Our collaborative definition of Emotional Literacy which highlights the need for individual understanding of ourselves and each other is significant when we consider the concerns of Christie et al. (1999), that the young people of Europe are disaffected, demonstrating a decline in social and moral values. Their evidence suggests that greater effort should be made to encourage preventative strategies aimed at promoting children's social skills and interpersonal awareness.

Christie et al. undertook an intervention study in Scottish primary schools using a sample of 321 9-year-old children. The findings of this study clearly highlight the potential of programmes which encourage Emotional Literacy. Perhaps never before in history has this concept of interpersonal awareness been more important. Set in a contemporary society where materialism at times seems to outweigh traditional values and where social respect appears to be in decline, Emotional Literacy encompasses so much which simply makes social common sense. With its roots in the interdisciplinary foundations of brain research, neurology, psychoneuroimmunology, educational research, psychotherapeutic research, psychiatric research and social and cognitive therapy, Emotional Literacy has a prestigious heritage. It brings together the work of Goleman (1996) with Gardner (1983), highlighting their common belief in the importance of recognising breadth of intelligences, in particular intrapersonal intelligence (understanding oneself) and interpersonal intelligence (understanding others). Now Emotional Literacy appears at the heart of our curriculum reforms, as stated in the Social and Emotional Aspects of Learning (DCSF, 2005).

Goleman (1996) suggests the potential that Emotional Literacy can offer to increase workplace effectiveness, personal wellbeing, confidence and mental health. How healthy we are, the relationships we build, the way we learn and behave are all influenced by our emotions. In fact Elias et al. (2003) claim that Emotional Literacy developed as a proactive strategy, promoting interpersonal awareness, is the missing piece in true educational reform and preparation for both academic and life success. Emotional Literacy may well facilitate raising attainment (Craczyk et al., 2000; Hallam et al., 2004; Zins et al., 2004), but more crucially it is believed to provide the foundation of a better society for the future. Knoll & Patti (2003: 39) allege that '*What we are as adults is a product of the world we experience as children*'.

The stated purpose of a Curriculum for Excellence (SEED, 2004) is to ensure that all the children of Scotland 'flourish' now and in the future. And within the context of the Welsh curriculum the vision is to ensure that all children and young people are listened to and treated with respect (DCELS, 2008).

The Problems with Emotional Literacy

You could be forgiven for considering whether this may be yet another 'band wagon' and like Carr (2000) or Smith (2003), suggest caution. Certainly the concept of Emotional Literacy has critics, for example Gott (2003). The research base supporting academic performance is inconsistent at best. In 2002 Weare & Gray carried out a review of English Local Education Authorities (LEA) which were at that time already committed to school emotional health programmes. Although they found marked improvements in behaviour, learning, confidence, social cohesion and academic achievement, there was no link proven to Emotional Literacy. In fact in their own evaluation they described their findings as 'embryonic' with results tending to be 'impressionistic'.

In a survey of over 700 research reports from Scottish schools, Topping & Homes (1998) found mixed and moderate success rates. A later overview by Topping et al. (2000) was even less positive. Mathews & Zeidner (2000: 460), in a study of empirical research on coping effectiveness, which is central to emotional literacy, claimed that it was *'overstated and unsupported by evidence'*. Donaldson-Feilder & Bond (2004), in studying UK workers, found levels of emotional intelligence did not predict wellbeing. Further concerns are also raised in Humpry et al. (2007) and Zeidner et al. (2002). However, Faupel (2003: 1) describes Emotional Literacy like a childhood memory of candy-floss which looks and tastes sweet, yet fills a lot of space without any real substance. Curiously he simultaneously pronounced himself proud to be leading the English intervention in Southampton LEA where Emotional Literacy was an educational priority, consciously linked to issues of inclusion and equal opportunity. This anomaly suggests that although Emotional Literacy may defy conventional measurement many schools which undertake this approach can feel the 'intangible' effects on their community.

To Think About:

- *Why are social and emotional skills essential in the workplace?*

The Significance of Emotional Literacy to Education

Against these doubts, the significance of Emotional Literacy is that it reflects a grassroots concern that schooling had lost its holism and become very narrow, focusing on the traditional academic view of education valued in terms of measurable academic achievements, attendance and exclusions (Weare, 2004). Rogers, writing in 1969 (p. vi), discussed the challenges facing contemporary education at that time and warned that *'it must prepare us to live responsibly and communicatively in an ever changing world of increasing international tensions'*. The recognition that schools can play a key role through promoting emotional wellbeing is increasing, a notion supported by Burton & Shotton (2004). The values and purposes underpinning the National Curriculum (DCSF, 2009) state that education must enable us to *'respond positively to the opportunities and challenges of the rapidly changing world in which we live and work'*.

The benefit I see in Emotional Literacy is through its interdisciplinary foundations which facilitate crossing curricular boundaries, permeating all disciplines within education and bringing together under the one umbrella, a broad range of educational issues. Together they have a common purpose in improving the quality of the school community. The vital personal and social skills of communication, empathy and self esteem can be taught through every curricular area. A holistic approach is strongly supported in the work of Gardner (1993), who advocates the importance of a broad and balanced curriculum. It is this very breadth, however, coupled with the difficulties in assessment, which are claimed ultimately to undermine the theory's scientific credence. Goleman (1996) in particular was criticised by Hedlund & Sternberg (2000: 146) for trying to *'capture almost everything but IQ'* in his definition of Emotional Literacy. However, in the Welsh Statutory Education Programme (DCELS, 2008: 14) which identifies seven areas of learning in the foundation stage 3–7 years, the first of these is Personal and Social Development, Wellbeing and Cultural Diversity which it states is *'at the heart of the Foundation Phase and should be developed across the curriculum'*.

What is being argued here is that Emotional Literacy may not be a fully proven construct, but the concept deals with real-life problems and is acknowledged at many different levels. To provide an opportunity to test out its validity within the curriculum the main resources required are simply curriculum flexibility, allocated time and teacher professionalism. If early intervention in literacy and number is important then surely it must be crucial in emotional understanding. Faupel (2002: 124) successfully explained that enabling children to live with others amiably while retaining feelings of self worth and simultaneously preserving the self esteem and confidence of others must be a core aim of education.

The original project hoped to demonstrate that personal and social development, in particular Emotional Literacy, not only belongs in the curriculum but in fact requires a similar central status to that given at present to the more tangible '3Rs'. Hargreaves (2000: 824) supported my rather idealistic proposal describing emotional understanding as *'a key criterion'* in teaching *'central to high standards good colleagueship and strong partnerships'*. Emotional Literacy should not be squashed into the periphery of the school day, but should be an equal partner with literacy and numeracy.

In fact when looking now at current education policy it is described as central to effective learning in A *Curriculum for Excellence*, Scotland (SEED, 2009) and as a core aim in the the Welsh curriculum (DCELS, 2008). At the time of writing my original project I believed that the government was paying lip service to the idea with little evidence of action, mainly due to the popular public belief that attainment was more important. Now the tide is turning and the new curriculum across the United Kingdom does indeed put health and wellbeing, including the emotional domain, at the heart of its policy along with numeracy and literacy – the big three. The values and purposes underpinning the national curriculum key stage 1 and 2 describe an educational pathway which leads to personal wellbeing (DCSF, 2009).

The Action Research Context

This project was based on the belief that education is child-centred in nature, on the premise that skills in Emotional Literacy are fundamental to becoming a full, active and valued member of society and that Emotional Literacy comes from within and is expressed through our communication and behaviours. Furthermore, it is perceived that these skills, initially developed in the home environment, are more developed in some children than others, depending on their socio-cultural circumstances, and can be nurtured within the school community to encourage communication, allow expression of feeling, develop understanding of others and build self control. My assertion is that development of Emotional Literacy skills through the growth of self awareness and self esteem will empower children to maximise their learning and thereby in time raise attainment. This is supported in the work of Morris (2002), Hargreaves (2000) and Goleman (1996, 1998).

After reflecting on current Emotional Literacy literature, along with considerable observation and reflection upon the social interactions within the nursery, I chose to undertake an action research approach to answer the research question:

> If Emotional Literacy becomes an explicit focus during the pre-school stage as part of daily small-group time and throughout the nursery activities, will this develop the children's ability to express their feelings, and to manage their own social behaviour?

Forming a Baseline

A firm and collaborative foundation was first established on which to build this project through:

- pupil observation, followed by staff team discussion, reflection, evaluation, planning and organisation, in line with the action research process (Altrichter et al., 1993)
- building strong relationships with the parents through daily exchanges of information and regular coffee meetings (Fullan, 1991)
- the introduction of daily group times with a focus on active listening and participation to build confidence and listening and talking skills (Bayley & Broadbent, 2001).

In addition data was gathered to form a triangulated baseline demonstrating an initial level of Emotional Literacy through:

- semi-structured interview, gathering quantitative data on pupil use of emotional vocabulary and supported by a parental questionnaire
- semi-structured interview, gathering quantitative data on pupil recognition and labelling of facial expression
- observation, gathering qualitative data on pupil social interaction.

These data gathering methods were discussed fully in the dissertation; together they formed both investigator and methodological triangulation for a baseline which demonstrated the quality of emotional vocabulary being used by the children.

The pupil emotional vocabulary interviews were carried out with consideration to justification and limitations using a semi-structured interview schedule as shown in Resource 1.5. This incorporated the use of a puppet who, having lost his voice needed the children's help. The objective was to ascertain if the children could verbalise an emotional understanding of how another would feel in a given scenario. The puppet was used to retain focus through making the activity both more fun and understandable for the younger age group. A questionnaire was also given out to all parents with the objective of supporting the data collected from the pupil interview through asking parents about the range of vocabulary that children use to express their emotional understanding of social situations. This questionnaire was based on the same interview scenarios as the children and to encourage questionnaire returns a discrete returns box was set up and a note of thanks combined with a reminder was distributed to maximise returns.

To establish the level of understanding of non-verbal communication the children were shown a series of characterised expression drawings within the form of a semi-structured interview. Use of a set of pictures rather than real expressions was considered by the nursery team to be a more consistent technique and less open to bias through individual presentation.

Observation data was collected through nursery narrative, video, audio and photographic observations during free play and small group-time activities. The objective was to reflect on the extent to which pupil vocabulary to express understanding of emotions impacts on their social behaviour, gauge pupil confidence to express their own feelings and opinions and to reflect on and develop the practical application of Emotional Literacy development in the classroom context.

Cohen et al. (2000: 113) assert that *'the weakness of any one method can be strengthened by using a combined approach to the problem'*. Through employing *'investigator triangulation'* to observation, a collaborative problem-solving approach was achieved. The action research approach best met our aim to reflect upon and monitor changes to practice, as a result of introducing Emotional Literacy within the nursery. It is an approach based on collaborative problem solving, which specifically suits nursery staffing and which Campbell et al. (2004: 22) claim encourages thriving *'professional communities'* and *'networks'*.

Why Action Research?

The beauty of action research in the early years context is its flexibility to adjust the project activities to meet the children's needs and interests in keeping with the early years framework. Somekh (1995: 340), writing in a comprehensive position paper for SCREE, sees it as *'designed to bridge the gap between research and practice'*. This design flexibility also facilitates the extension of the project into the first year of school. Furthermore, Emotional Literacy has proved difficult to assess (Mathews et al., 2002; Cole et al., 2004), particularly with young children, and action research lends itself to a more child-centred, qualitative basis of analysis. Hargreaves (1992) claims that the process promotes a positive climate, enhances teacher practice and thereby raises pupil attainment.

To ensure purposeful reflection I used the process of discussion with 'critical friends' as described in Campbell et al. (2004). This support helped to retain a certain perspective when as a teacher researcher one can become deeply involved in the learning and teaching process. I believe that the learning gained through the action research process is particularly strong and at the top quality end of the Rogers & Freiberg (1995) continuum of experiential learning. Elliot & Sarland (1995: 384) conclude that action research *'is now established as an important and influential movement'* bringing about what Elliot (1991: 52) describes as *'practical wisdom'*.

To Think About:

- *What are the benefits to be gained from reflecting on your practice?*

A major component and benefit integral to the effective action research process is the regular recording of reflections in the form of a journal. These reflections should be both constructive and objective, used to inform next steps, to initiate change and improve practice. Holly & Mcloughlin (1989) assert that the writing process slows thinking and makes it more effective. The deeper learning gained through this reflection process facilitates metacognition, creating opportunity for professional development and flexibility and openness to new ideas, characteristic of learning at higher levels.

A reflective journal based on personal observations of practice, and which also relates reflections to professional reading and development opportunities, facilitates the action research process through conscientious and meaningful reflection. This choice of research vehicle is central to the action research process, and can generate a deep and rich data source. Although this type of data can create some difficulties in drawing together a clear and concise analysis, the advantage of the flexible, child-centred, informal approach allows for personal feeling and opinion. The data generated is invaluable so long as it is recognised for what it is, opinion which is based on experience. Somekh (1995) supports the assertion that documentation of reflections affords validity to the research.

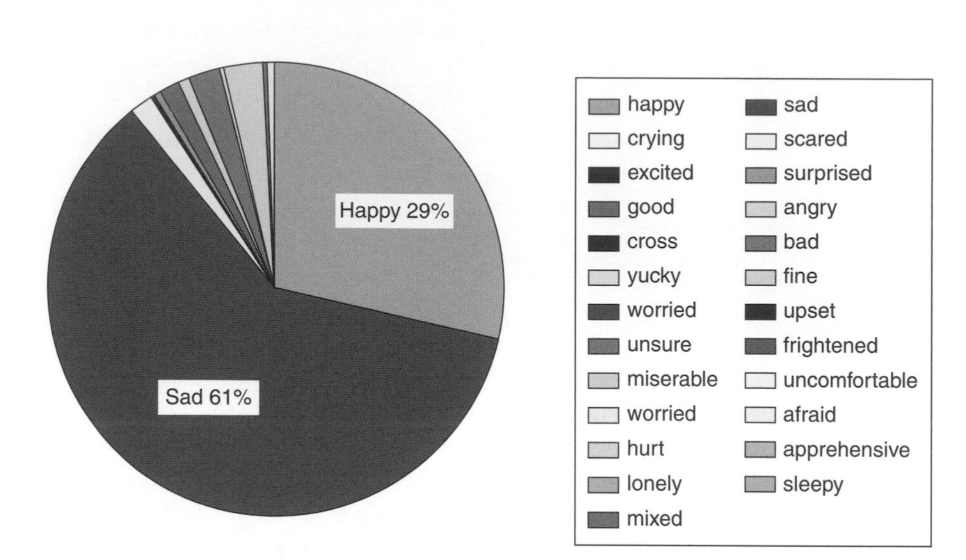

Figure 1.3 Results of the emotional vocabulary pupil interview

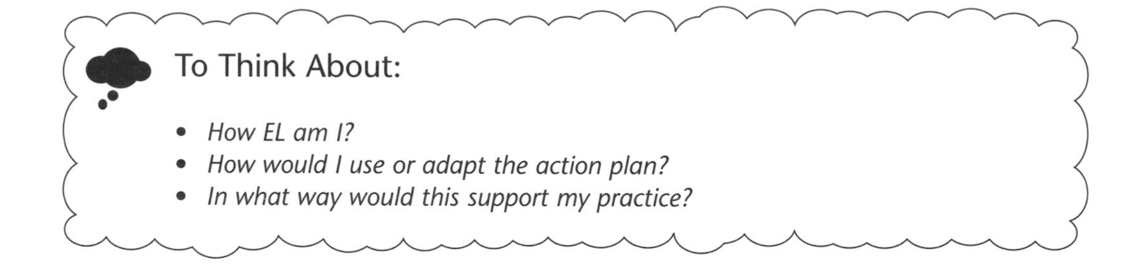

The baseline data results of the pupil emotional vocabulary interviews gave a very clear picture of the children's limited vocabulary to express emotions, 90% of the responses given being either sad or happy (Figure 1.3). This could simply have been due to immaturity, but it seemed highly probable that a lack of encouragement to use a more expansive vocabulary had played an important part.

Since most children from the age of 3 are now in highly social pre-school environments, this skill is required to cope with the increased demands in social convention and interactions in their lives. In this case a nursery initiative to increase pupil vocabulary would be likely to show improved results. Reflections on the initial findings from the parents' questionnaire suggested that parents are often unaware of the pressures upon their children and gave me cause to reflect more deeply on those who struggle with separation and the process of induction into nursery, unable to express how they are feeling appropriately.

The data from the parents' questionnaire which was originally intended to support the data collection within the nursery, supported these reflections. Happy and sad responses this time made up only 36% of the total vocabulary used. The diverse range of emotional vocabulary collected here was based on the same scenarios as the pupil

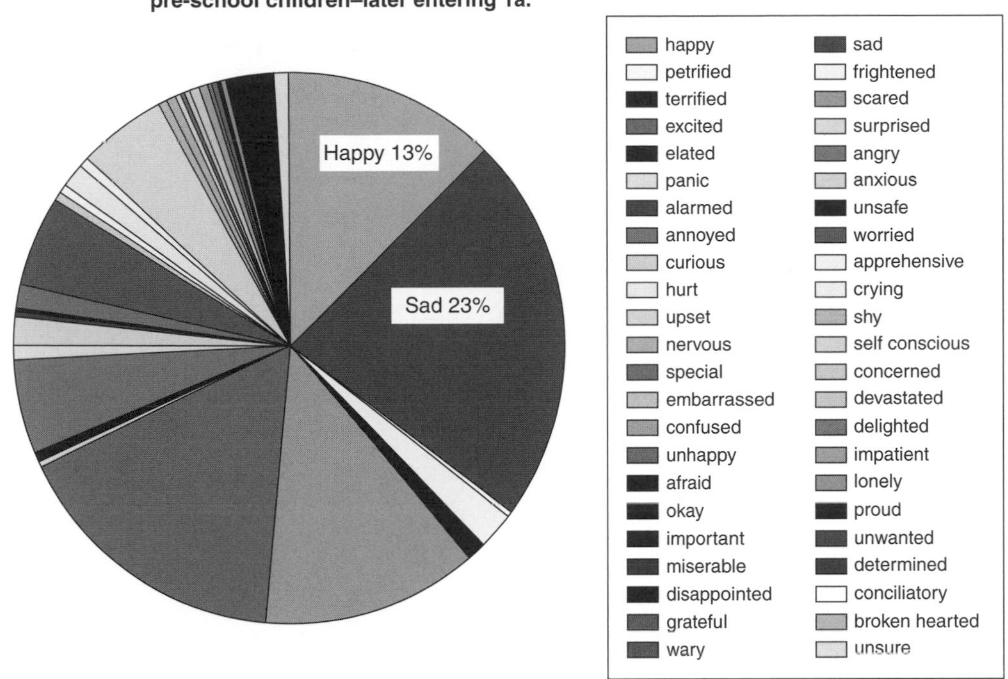

Figure 1.4 Results of the emotional vocabulary parent questionnaire, January

interviews and asked the parents which words they thought their *children* would use to describe how they would feel in the presented circumstances (Figure 1.4). The obvious discrepancy supports the assertion that parents are indeed unaware of the limitations of their children's expressive vocabulary.

An Action Plan

I realised through a process of reading and reflection on the initial data findings, the limited ability of our children to express both their own emotional understanding and that of their peers. A clear picture formed which contrasted with the ethos of the nursery. It also suggested that adults, including the nursery team, had a limited appreciation not only of the children's perspective but their own levels of Emotional Literacy. Data collected suggested that our children often simply did not have the internal language to understand, or the vocal language to express what they were feeling, resorting either to aggression or withdrawal. Support can be found for this in Ladd & Burgess (1999). Building on these reflections the action plan to monitor and embed Emotional Literacy into the nursery curriculum was refined, and in this way the action research cycle initiated.

In Chapter 2, I will go on to discuss how to organise an emotionally literate environment through some simple but effective changes to practice and how to get an Emotional Literacy project up and running.

Further Reading

The New Meaning of Educational Change by Michael Fullan (2007), originally published in 1991, is now in its 4th edition and has useful advice concerning the impact and sustainability of change, as does *Breakthrough* written by the same author in 2006.

Developing the Emotionally Literate School written by Katherine Weare (2004) gives an excellent overview. I only regret it was not available when I was carrying out my project.

I also recently read *Why Love Matters: How Affection Shapes a Baby's Brain* by Sue Gerhardt (2004). This is a very interesting background read underlining the significance of early relationships on later social behaviours.

Electronic Resources

Go to www.sagepub.co.uk/chrstinebruce for electronic resources for this chapter:

1.1 Project Aims and Objectives

1.2 Project Action Plan

1.3 Project Timetable

1.4 Revised Timetable

1.5 Nursery Pupil Interview

1.6 Primary Pupil Interview

1.7 Nursery Parent Interview

1.8 Primary Parent Interview

1.9 Emotional Expression Drawings

Emotional Literacy as an Approach to Learning and Teaching

In this chapter, I consider:

- **How small changes in your practice can have a big impact**
- **Creating and using spaces for Emotional Literacy**
- **Planning for Emotional Literacy.**

Previously, I gave a flavour of the context for the project, the initial research planning and baseline findings. These were based on considerable observation and reflection upon the social interactions within the nursery and gave rise to the action research question:

> If Emotional Literacy becomes an explicit focus during the pre-school stage as part of daily small-group time and throughout the nursery activities, will this develop the children's ability to express their feelings, and to manage their own social behaviour?

I also put forward the notion that Emotional Literacy is a way of being, not just of doing. It is a pedagogical approach concerning teaching style and learning environment. Now consider how this might affect your practice as your read on.

The development of Emotional Literacy in this project was based on a series of common threads in my reading but was strongly influenced by the person-centred ideals of Rogers (1969) and inspired by the practical success of Sharp (2001) and Faupel (2003). These ideas stress the importance of establishing a sense of belonging, through using small groups to teach specific skills within a supportive framework. This unified and empathetic approach depends on a common teaching and learning philosophy, which puts Emotional Literacy centrally in the curriculum, developing self esteem and greater pupil autonomy. Underlying this is the work of Hanko (2002) and Roberts (1995). Undertaking action research allowed this approach to develop and grow in depth as I continued to read and reflect on a variety of experiences. In this chapter, I hope to share some of the ideas which, as they come together, underpin the EL approach.

How Small Changes Can Have a Big Impact

An Emotional Literacy approach recognises the basic principles of good teaching while making small but significant changes to practice. Neurologists have now demonstrated that quality of learning is significantly affected by our experiences and learning environment (Greenfield, 2000). To start and then maintain a learning environment built on Emotional Literacy means approaching your class organisation and planning with Emotional Literacy foremost in your mind. I suggest whatever the stage of your pupils, that you involve them in the setting up of their working environment. Working from a roughly drawn plan, first form a skeleton organisation with the heavier furniture, I like to try drawing out several ideas first before I start lugging heavy furniture about. It's also a good idea to put the chairs out of the way before you start so that you are not constantly tripping over them. To support the very young, strategically place some items which suggest an area use. Basic common sense rules here! Much of this plan, which incorporates your main gathering or teaching area, will come down to what you feel comfortable working with; however, I find there are some definite must-haves for the primary classroom, for example:

- A seat for each child where the board can be seen clearly from, they can work in collaborative groups and yet have their own personal space

- Clear easy access to the exit, resources and pupils, their personal belongings and enough space to generally move around the room. Children need their own space to feel happy working together. If they are constantly bumping into each other or a bottle neck forms at key transition times then this causes friction.

Discuss the practicalities with the children and ask them to help in planning the learning or activity areas which they would like in their class. Hammond (2007) believes if we truly want to put children at the centre of learning then we must learn to listen to their suggestions about the environments in which they want to learn at the planning stage. They will be happy to tell you which resource spaces and labels are needed in the classroom. Older children can work together to map or plan their ideas on A1 sheets. Then, with discussion, put together the best planning ideas and share the responsibilities for their upkeep. This gives the children ownership and responsibility for their class and for organising the seating too. Asking the children's opinion is time consuming and, as Hammond (2007) would agree, seldom straightforward, but we can learn and observe so much from them. She found children favoured natural elements such as sand or mud, learning actively through real and rich experiences. An Emotionally Literate approach and environment encourage active learning.

Chill Time

We live in a world full of noise, traffic, mobile phones, MP3s, radio and television, just for a start. I like to teach our children to appreciate how different sounds affect our mood and to hear the sounds of nature and quiet too. A useful time to build this into the day is directly after lunch when a 10-minute slot of meditation, quiet reflection, silent reading or story can be built in. This can be supported through gentle, quiet music. I call this chill time, a really useful time to refocus on afternoon expectations and naturally this needs some flexibility within the daily timetable.

Different learning spaces add interest and warmth to your learning environment. I appreciate that creating an exciting and stimulating classroom environment is not a new idea, but this goes beyond the physical environment and focuses on the style of discourse. Connecting learning to the children's lives and modifying the teaching approach in ways that are more interactive, engaging and meaningful for pupils creates a positive mood which, as Harris (2007) tells us, deepens learning.

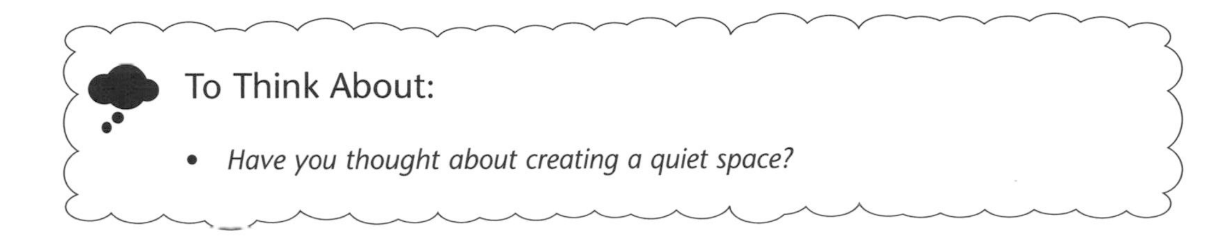

Developing and Using Space

A Quiet Space

Within the structure of your newly created learning environment also allow a space for solitary chill or cool down. This could be a floor area with a rug and cushion, a den made with an old sheet or a specific table with two chairs. This designated space should be kept specifically for the purpose of quiet reflection with an alternative general use quiet area elsewhere for reading and/or writing activities. Give careful thought to how you will resource this space, for example a very young child may feel exhausted after a tantrum whereas an older child may benefit from a copy of your class contract (see resource bank) with paper and pencil to hand, a 1–10 emotion chart or an emotion management book ... I find a reflective writing journal ideal support for older children.

Space for Emotional Literacy

Small areas for curricular resource and display, for example devoted to science, free writing, reading, listening, small world play, topic work, are applicable within the learning area for any age group to stimulate thinking, discussion and challenge. So why not a specific area for emotional literacy resourced with a mirror, emotion management books, pencils, a class journal, worry box, post-its. This would be a 'thinking space' for reflection on events. A wall of fame to celebrate success and express feelings of pride might support this area as well as a special person chart which gives each child the opportunity to be a special person for the day. I display their photo with some thoughts as to why they are special added from the children. The class can decide at the beginning of term what the special day right or rights might be, for example line leader, responsibility for the class puppet, use of a particular cushion, the right to sit anywhere or in a special chair, etc.

Photo 2.1 A tent for a quiet den

Photo 2.2 A place to sit and think

Your Space

The teacher's desk, so often piled up with classroom rubble, should not be excluded from this EL environment. This is an opportunity to set an example to the children. The surface should be tidy and calming with a photo of the class family along with

Photo 2.3 EL nursery display

Photo 2.4 EL year 1 display

one of your family and perhaps flowers or a plant. A colourful basket or box could be used to store miscellaneous teaching aids such as a task timer, positive smiley face or star shaped post-its to hand out, your daily plan with space to jot down reflections and observations as you work. Encourage any class visitor or support staff to add their observations too.

T:	*I was a wonderful 10 at breakfast time 'cause my mummy said L and R could come to play with me tonight but now I feel a number 1 'cause she got mixed up, I've got dancing so they can't come and now I'm miserable.*
R: Me: R:	*I'm at number 10 because it's sunny and I like being with my friends.* *How was your sister last night?* *I'm proud of my sister 'cause she stops crying when I ask her to.*
	OR
A:	*I feel yellow and fantastic 'cause it's sunny and I like playing football outside.*
B:	*I feel green, it's not fair, I wanted to stay home and play with my cousin.*

Figure 2.1 4½–5 year old children express their emotional state using a number or colour

'Our' Space

Welcome and start the day with clear organisational routines. When you open the door in the morning welcome not just the children, but their parents and families too. Part of that routine are the class greetings which help to establish a sense of belonging and community. This is an opportunity to express a personal emotional state using a number or colour (see Figure 2.1).

The EL classroom belongs to each child as well as the teacher so why not have everybody's name or photo on the door – not just the teachers. Consider too the first thing that visitors will see as they come in through the door. What will be facing them? Is it something attractive, interesting or maybe interactive?

As the day ends prepare the learning environment for the next day with the children. Signal the start of this new tidying and preparation time with some specific music (a tidy-up song can help here too). Before everyone goes home gather together and celebrate the day. How do you feel today went? What did we learn today? What did you enjoy most? What will we be doing tomorrow?

The Teaching Space

This should be a carpeted space big enough for the whole class to sit together and preferably big enough for a circle activity. It's very useful to have a big book stand and space to display objects of interest. I always have one or two of what I call **Community puzzle bags** to hand. These might contain lotto cards for finding learning partners, 'I am' cards for number games, a giant jigsaw to share the pieces, or a beanie to throw and name. An **Emergency bag** might contain putty for a fidget, a cold shiny shell or a small soft beanie for a restless child to hold still in both their hands and keep safe.

Planning for Emotional Literacy

When planning in both the longer term and on a day-to-day basis, health and wellbeing should permeate across the curriculum. What better way to cover many of the health and wellbeing aspects than through an Emotionally Literate approach where

Photo 2.5 A teacher's desk should be tidy and attractive

Photo 2.6 A classroom belongs to a class, so have everybody's name on the door

the importance of establishing belonging cannot be over-emphasised in supporting positive behaviour and quality learning (Gerhardt, 2004). If you are planning from an Emotionally Literate perspective then the needs of your children will be at the heart of your planning. You will consider the environment which suits their learning needs, how they learn best and their personal interests. However, as Hammond (2007) states, if children are truly at the core of the planning process you will honestly listen to their voices and opinions. This means you are working in partnership with your pupils and requires a thorough knowledge and respect for the children, their needs and interests. As previously stated, asking a child's opinion may be time consuming, but it is well worth making that extra effort to encourage active engagement in learning.

To Think About:

- *How much do I really know about my pupils?*
- *How could I find out?*

Relationships

An Emotionally Literate approach is sensitive to the individual needs of children and their need to have a sense of belonging and of group identity. This is a basic human need which can be achieved through developing confident communication skills. To be ignored by our parents or teachers is essentially emotional abuse, which triggers undesirable emotions. More than one in every 20 children regularly suffer from attacks on their emotional wellbeing and self confidence, including frequent violence between parents, regular humiliation, threat, and being told their parents wish they'd never been born (Cawson et al., 2000). As early as 1985, Grossmann found that the quality of exchange between an infant and their parent or 'attachment figure' was crucial in developing both communication and emotional expression, which in turn affect social competence and emotional wellbeing. Today the quality of relationships in a class, particularly between teacher and pupil are widely recognized as underpinning all learning. Sometimes relationship is considered to be the fourth 'R', after reading, writing and arithmetic. The skills of friendship need to be discussed and specifically taught, often through one of the many useful stories which are on the market. The web-based Resource 2.1 lists some of my personal favourites and I'm sure you could add many more.

To support building relationships it is very useful when children are starting nursery or primary school to ask parents for some background information. This is often easily achieved through a questionnaire asking families about their child's favourite foods, interests, likes and dislikes. This is something that you can suggest parents and children do together, perhaps their first homework task which the children can help with through drawing. This information gives you a starting point for discussion and for getting to know your pupil. The web-based Resource 2.2 holds a downloadable worksheet which I have used with various ages to support this process.

Class Contracts

Another important step is to build an EL class contract with the children for a place where we can all feel safe, feel confident and feel relaxed. The teacher can scribe for the youngest children who can then illustrate their work but everyone, whatever their age, should sign or make their mark on the contract. A copy of the contract should also go home with each child with an opportunity for the parent to read, discuss and comment. An example of a contract can be found in Resource 2.3.

Developing Resilience and Discipline

An Emotionally Literate approach is very effective in matters of discipline. Again, whatever the age of the child the adult approach would be to encourage the children as far as is possible to take responsibility for sorting out the matter themselves, and I include the rest of the class or bystanders here: 'How does that make you [them] feel?' 'What do you think you [they] need to do?' 'Do you think that is a fair solution?' Encourage children to take responsibility for correcting their mistakes and developing their understanding of the feelings of others and how they feel when they take control of their behaviour. This teaches and then supports the practicing of skills for resilience in a safe environment. Consider carefully the language adults often model, for example distracting a child and often confusing them by saying something is not sore when through our own experience we know that it is! This principle is further discussed in Chapter 5.

When there have been behaviour issues take time to reflect and discuss these with the children and your colleagues. Find out where they happen, when and why. One approach which you might consider with a class is to stop for break five or 10 minutes early and go outside with your children. You will benefit from some fresh air and movement, but this also shows that you value break time as an important part of the school day. In your pocket carry what I describe as 'instant fun', for example bubbles or streamers, see the web-based Resource 4.5 for more expanded ideas.

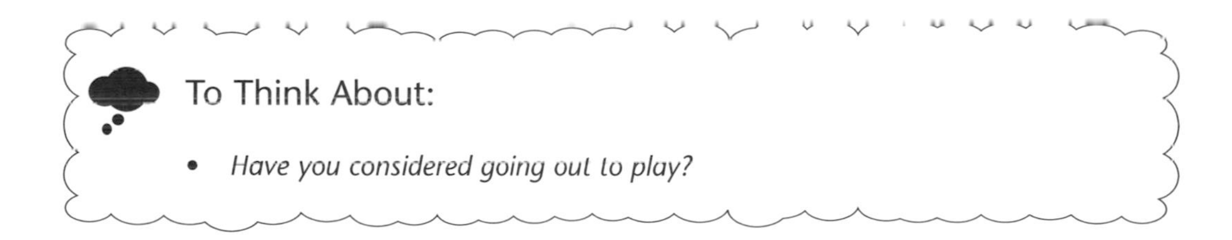

Achieving Quality Learning

Developing Emotional Literacy is believed by many to raise academic achievement through an approach which is sensitive to the child's needs (Elias et al., 2003; Sheppy, 2009). As adults we have all experienced stress, with our emotions out of control, our brain in overload. Not only does our memory suffer but the power to systematically reason out problems also suffers. Research in neuroscience has centred on the role of the prefrontal cortex, the part of the brain just behind the forehead, which develops most rapidly between the ages of 3 and 8. This area manages our instinctive emotional impulses, which come from the amygdala, redirecting powerful feelings, such as fear, straight to all major centres of the brain. As previously stated in Chapter 1 (page 3), it is also involved in cognitive, social and emotional processes such as the regulation of attention, planning, self control, flexibility and self awareness. Goleman (1996) purports that the physiology of the brain means that learning and strong emotion compete for space in working memory. Both positive and negative feelings have an influence on learning, memory and problem solving skills as well as how we relate to others.

This information is of crucial importance in supporting educators since it suggests that to achieve quality learning we must first deal with the emotions. Rogers (1969) purports that real effective learning is facilitated by teachers when they listen to pupils' feelings with sensitivity, respect and acceptance of pupil worth, demonstrating empathetic understanding with the pupils' perspective. If quality of learning is a continuum, then to achieve the very best quality involves active, experiential learning in a positive learning environment, which develops skills in independence and responsibility through communication and group work (Damasio, 2003).

Organising Teaching

Similar to more traditional ideas of literacy, Emotional Literacy begins by breaking learning down into simple concepts and skills and progresses to more complex interpersonal abilities (see Figure 1.2, page 5). In considering the practicalities of the planned nursery intervention within the stated pressures of the curriculum, a simple formulaic approach using a prescriptive programme of study which develops communication skills might appear to be a tempting answer, but would it be sufficient to effect change in itself?

What Would Be the Best Way to Go About It?

Dyer (2002), in 'A "Box Full of Feelings"', concluded that Emotional Literacy, and indeed all learning, is an interactive, life-long process which cannot be achieved in isolation. However, Savage (2001) reports on the progress of a successful project which used **the nurture group approach** to support inclusion of year 1 pupils with emotional and behavioural difficulties. This approach, pioneered by Bennathan & Boxall (1996), was significantly modified to *withdraw* a small group with a support assistant for 30 minutes daily. The aim was to develop the children's listening skills, independence and readiness to learn within the context of the supportive group. There are also a growing number of schools which withdraw regular groups for anger management. These groups, led by dedicated support staff, have experienced substantial success (Faupel, 2003; Burton & Shotton, 2004). Cooper & Tiknazy (2005), however, warn that an imbalance of one problem in a group can be counterproductive and reinforce the group characteristics.

Small focus groups may be most effective when they are set alongside the powerful peer pressure associated with a whole-school or nursery approach. This notion of pupil empowerment through developing a sense of belonging provided good reason to involve all the pupils in small groups within our project. Central to this is the concept of holism and the potential of Emotional Literacy in establishing a supportive climate conducive to learning and teaching. This is built on the principle of inclusion, developing a sense of understanding, belonging and self esteem, all of which have a common foundation in communication skills. It was for these reasons that within our project we worked with small groups to develop communication

Record what is happening: what the child can do. **Date/time:**
Straight description – no interpretation.

S observing a game going on in the house corner. He is standing in the background by the screen quietly watching. No interaction with the other children. No facial expression or gesture observed.

+10 mins: Just continues to stand and watch unnoticed by the group. Goes off on his own to the story corner when the story bell rings.

Is he absorbed in their world?

Figure 2.2 Excerpt from a baseline observation demonstrating lack of communication

skills initially through the resource Baseline Communication (Delamain & Spring, 2000), while using the action research process to reflect on pupil progress and my own practice in order to extend the principles of Emotional Literacy throughout the nursery activities. We could then work to improve the self esteem, behaviour and learning motivation of the individual child. I believe this is how 'attainment' will ultimately be reached. The effect may not be immediately measurable yet some of our greatest educational theorists such as Vygotsky would support this philosophy.

How Would I Know if Change Made a Difference?

If you want to prove that your initiative has made a difference to learning then you will need a starting point or baseline of initial knowledge, as outlined in Chapter 1, with which to measure or compare your progress. In this case the initial data findings formed a clear picture of the limited ability of the children at that time, to express both their own emotional understanding and that of their peers, with 90% of the responses given being either sad or happy (see Figure 1.3 on page 13). We considered the ability to use expressive language particularly important in developing social skills and resilience and were concerned about the limitations of the children's expressive vocabulary. The initial data also suggested adults, including the nursery team, had a limited appreciation of not only the children's perspective but their own levels of Emotional Literacy (see Figure 1.4 on page 13). Our initial pupil observations, taken as part of the baseline, were focused on skills in social interaction, as supported in Cole et al. (2004). The exercise raised concern about the number of children who appeared quiet and withdrawn. There is an example observation given in Figure 2.2.

Children with this type of problem can often become invisible in a busy environment, a problem which Weare & Gray (2002) acknowledge. Reflecting on our observations we decided to use the observed levels of interaction as the criteria to form our initial small groups. This meant that the children, regardless of age or academic ability, could be supported, and support each other, in establishing a sense of belonging and in building self esteem.

The importance of establishing the ability to 'read' non-verbal communication became apparent during team discussion and reflection of the initial observations of pupil interaction, where we found this had been commonly observed as a precursor to social misunderstandings. This is supported in the research of McGinley (2001) who also found children with difficulty expressing their feelings verbally tended towards more physical expression. Klein (2001) reports that children when they are out of control, frightened and unable to explain, become disruptive, aggressive or withdrawn.

In fact most of our observations of 4-year-olds in play contexts demonstrated concern for upset peers, but this did not seem to extend to an understanding of why they felt as they did. Neither did they appear to pick up on the more subtle signals when other children were not experiencing the same feeling as themselves, that is, no longer finding their behaviour fun.

Keeping a Reflective Journal

The importance of reflection on practice is now seen across education as empowering and a vital component in supporting the development of our teaching skills. It is based on your personal philosophy, the values and beliefs which underpin your teaching. As Farrell (2004) highlights, experience itself is not the greatest teacher, we learn much more when we question and reflect on that experience. Conversely, teachers who do not undertake reflection on their practice become entrenched and stagnate; it is far easier to complain about the system or the behaviour than to undertake personal reflection. A reflective journal based on personal observations of practice, and which also relates reflections to professional reading and development opportunities, as explained in Chapter 1, supports not only pupil progress but improves the quality of teaching and learning.

For pre-school practitioners, recording observations for later reflection is a natural process. The team will meet daily to discuss, evaluate and to plan next steps. It is then a small step to also reflect on teaching and scaffolding opportunities. This open systematic process is less natural to many teachers/practitioners in the early school years, but why should this practice stop at the end of nursery? It could easily be a part of classroom practice and is well worth developing with colleagues. If the diary/plan is open on your desk anyone in the room can be encouraged to jot down comments or observations for later reflection. Discussion and evaluation of early years organisation, activities and practice can allow the action research process to build, and through sharing reflection on practice, to improve both teaching and learning. Using these observations to inform reflections is an important part of action research and a process which I find very calming and refreshing. See Figure 2.3 for an example of a series of journal entries.

As stated in Chapter 1, this project is based on the belief that education is child-centred in nature, on the premise that skills in Emotional Literacy are fundamental to becoming a full, active and valued member of society and that Emotional Literacy comes from within and is expressed through our communication and behaviour. Furthermore, these skills, initially developed in the home environment, are more developed in some children than others depending on their socio-cultural circumstances, and can be nurtured within the school community to encourage communication, allow expression of feeling, develop understanding of others and build self control. My assertion is that development of Emotional Literacy skills through the growth of self awareness and self esteem will empower children to maximise their

Taken from journal entry 19th April.
Dealing with a behaviour incident – G knocked down a patiently built tower.
**That worked well – but what did I do differently? Rather than asking him why did you do that?
I asked... How do you think X felt? He spent a long time building it. And … How do you feel now?
I asked the group – What do you think G should do? – Do you think G feels sorry? Well let's help him … and make it fun!*

Later I wrote:

**I'm taking a different perspective or angle!! It was more EL and it worked. I did make G stop & think. The other children were able to advise what to do and G did take responsibility. Group pressure at its best!!*

Taken from journal entry 20th April.
*Took more photos of gesture and expression during dramatic play today. Some nice contrasts between those who can and those who cannot – * Why? Is it the camera? Do some children put on special effects?? Are others deliberately avoiding expressions being caught on film?*

Later I wrote:

**… Could try videoing? It might be more natural and less intrusive!*

Taken from journal entry 21st April
A good pick up today – Mum had been a bit annoyed! I judged it right by simply giving a little more time – and it went down well! Is my EL improving? Spent time with Mum admiring photographs and so smoothing ruffled feathers. Time well spent!

Later:

*Is it understanding feelings? OR Understanding language to express feelings?
We require language to demonstrate the understanding – which is modelled through EL activities in nursery. We are giving the experience/practice within a secure environment e.g. I told them a scary fairy tale – letting the children experience scariness in safety and explore the relevant vocabulary. Let's keep developing stories this week and use the mystery contents box to build more stories – video children's reactions!*

Taken from journal entry 23rd April
Again this question – what does language prove? Do we have the same understandings? Conventions? Raised my concern – are reflections tight and deep enough! Useful word 'Permeates' – I used this a lot today. Should I add to the research question? To improve my reflections I will try using Critical Skills from reading David Tripp (1993).

Figure 2.3 A series of journal entries

learning and thereby in time raise attainment. This is supported in the work of Morris (2002), Hargreaves (2000) and Goleman (1996, 1998).

In this chapter we have looked at how little changes in your outlook and practice can have a huge impact. In Chapter 3, I will go on to discuss how we can improve our support for individual children within an Emotionally Literate classroom environment.

Further Reading

Behaviour Management, 2nd edition (2007) by Bill Rogers. There are many books on classroom behaviour management, but this must be one of the best in promoting positive behaviour.

Freedom to Learn by Carol Rogers & Jerome Freiberg is an inspiring read taking a person-centred approach to education, building discipline and classroom management with the learner and is now in its 3rd updated edition (1995).

Electronic Resources

Go to www.sagepub.co.uk/christinebruce for electronic resources for this chapter:

2.1 List of Stories for Encouraging Discussion

2.2 Transition Sheet: About Me

2.3 Example of Emotional Literacy Class Contract

2.4 'How I Feel' Worksheet

How an Emotionally Literate Approach can Support Inclusion

In this chapter, I consider:

- **The way current policy on inclusion affects schools**
- **How Emotional Literacy can support inclusion.**

I would ask you to first review your understandings of the definition of inclusion towards one which encompasses all children (Todd, 2007; Frederickson & Cline, 2009). All children are unique and experience barriers to learning at some point in their education; it is our responsibility to break down these barriers. This is a shift in thinking away from '*integration*', as the expectation that the child will cope with the existing learning environment if given support. Here '*inclusion*' means that we change our practice and learning environment to meet the needs of the child. Hamill & Clark (2005) acknowledge that putting these principles into practice is not easy and requires a conscious effort to counter the often unconscious discriminations each of us hold. As educators we have a moral responsibility to reflect on, and rise above, our own prejudice, to be aware of the hidden curriculum which we all project. The sense of values which we convey in our attitude, body language and demeanour, our whole approach to handling trivial, or perhaps not so trivial incidents, adds to the overall ethos. For me real inclusion has meant accepting children just the way they are!!

To Think About:

- *What do I think inclusion means?*
- *What difference do social skills make to inclusion?*

The way society thinks about education is ever changing, perhaps never more so than now. Inclusion is very much at the forefront of our minds in the teaching community and whatever your personal view, the law upholds the current drive for a more inclusive society. We have a duty to provide mainstream education for all children, except in certain circumstances (SENDA, 2001; Education Scotland Act, 2004) which could be interpreted as those with the most complex needs. This has in turn heaped expectations onto schools to find ways to meet and support the diverse needs of children so that they may succeed both academically and socially. This creates a requirement that many teachers find a major challenge. Support for this view is to be found in Cooper (2008: 13), which states *'No other educational problem is associated with such a level of frustration, fear, anger, guilt and blame'*. Evans & Lunt (2002: 5) warn that there is a growing voice of concern among policy makers about the number of children who are being excluded from schools, mainly for disruptive behaviour.

Perhaps to counter this there has been a substantial shift in education policy which asserts the central importance of emotional health and wellbeing in the curriculum across the United Kingdom. The values which underpin the National Curriculum Framework in England, Wales and the Scottish Curriculum for Excellence hold this at their core. As Todd (2007) points out, collaborative working to promote well-being and inclusive education is mentioned at least 40 times in *Every Child Matters* (DFES, 2004).

In support, Elias et al. (2003) purport that the social and emotional skills of Emotional Literacy are essential for democratic citizenship and to sustain relationships which support effective inclusion. This incorporation at the heart of education policy suggests greater emphasis on the concept of educating the 'whole child'. I also believe that success should not be the product of luck or privilege, but rather education has a moral responsibility to meet the challenges of a modern inclusive society. In Scotland the new curriculum is underpinned by the four values inscribed on the mace of the Scottish Parliament – wisdom, justice, compassion and integrity.

However, academic achievement for every child will never be realised through the more traditional notion of subject timetabling. There is no doubt that schools need to be accountable, with a more cohesive and inclusive structure 3–18, yet the resulting position is still an imbalance, with top-down pressure to meet academic targets apparent even in our nursery and foundation classes. The restrictions of timetabling, along with a constant requirement to provide material evidence of attainment, have left little room for developing social skills or Emotional Literacy. It is with immense relief therefore that I welcome the genuine signs of change that accompany the Early Years Framework (EYF) in Scotland and Early Years Foundation Stage (EYFS) Framework across the country. The EYFS curriculum guidance asserts that personal social and emotional development is critical in underpinning success in all aspects of learning and indeed the Social and Emotional Aspects of Learning (SEAL) underpin the whole primary framework.

To Think About:

- *What does inclusion mean in my class?*

Creating an Oasis for Children with Social, Emotional and Behavioural Needs

To manage successful inclusion requires the flexibility of time to take an Emotional Literate Approach (ELA) to daily organisation. On arrival each morning, children need time to adjust to school routines and to find peace within themselves before they can make room for learning. Each child carries with them issues of personal 'baggage' from home. The breakfast table arguments or scenes from the evening before don't automatically disappear the moment a child walks through your door! We all know that it is not until a child feels safe and secure in their environment that they will be able to open up to the challenges of learning. The result of an inflexible timetable can, as Cooper (2004) suggests, actually increase feelings of stress and exclusion, the resulting downhill spiral simply aggravating the barriers children face when approaching learning. The current emphasis on academic standards and achievements has sent out a strong anti-inclusive message suggesting that worth and value depends on academic achievement. However, Faupel (2002) states *'Human worth does not depend on what we do but on the fact that we are!'*

To combat these challenges to inclusion it is crucial to develop an inner awareness and sense of self. Self awareness and self esteem should be considered core elements in the development of Emotional Literacy. Consider the now well known adage 'Feel good, learn good'. Children with sound self esteem are more resilient in overcoming the risks and challenges which all learning involves. However, troubled children use much of their emotional energy to cope with their personal problems leaving less free energy to devote to learning, with frustration often manifesting in challenging behaviours.

To Think About:

- *What do you see as the main barrier to inclusion?*

Our task as teachers therefore is to use our understanding of Emotional Literacy to provide a smooth transition into each and every school day. Even more, to smooth the transitions within the day and at the day's end. If we keep this notion first and foremost in our minds as we plan our lessons, organise our learning environments and teach our children, we will achieve that desired oasis where children can find the inner confidence to enjoy the challenges and excitement of learning. Wrigley (2005: 32) describes a school community where *'young people can enjoy being together ... where learning embodies empathy and caring as well as intellectual scrutiny'*. This is our aim.

In 30 years of teaching I have never met two children with identical support needs, therefore there is no one-size-fits-all method or strategy. Supporting a child with emotional and behavioural needs is a complex balance between supporting social interaction with their peers and focused one-to-one teaching.

My best advice for creating a learning environment which is an inclusive oasis is simple – take time to establish a sense of belonging. Create a place where each individual develops their personal Emotional Literacy and looks out for each and every other individual. The EYFS Principle 1.4 states *'Babies and children have emotional well-being when their needs are met and their feelings are accepted. They enjoy relationships that are close, warm and supportive'.* (DCSF, 2008)

So, take time to ...

- Be there with a cheerful welcome come rain or shine – why not put your coat on and go out to greet the children?
- Allow a flexible or 'soft start' to the day where children can arrive in class 10 minutes before bell time and the working day begins.
- Listen to your children and make each child feel that what they have to say is of importance. Value every contribution.
- Create a welcoming ambience through lighting, scent, and music.
    - Try to use natural light whenever possible. Florescent lighting is very harsh, the glare creating a visual barrier to some children's learning.
    - Our sense of smell triggers strong emotional connections with our past experiences. Try using a vanilla 'plug-in' air freshener, although an aromatherapy humidifier would be much better.
    - Sounds around us also evoke strong emotional connections and a settling mood is easily created through soothing music. Similarly the introduction of bright and happy morning music can signal the change to working mode.
- Involve the children, in discussing, making and using five simple, clear, firm but fair rules for an Emotionally Literate class (see Resource 2.3 for an example).
- Develop clear routines using supporting picture cards and social stories (Gray, 2002; Whitehead, 2007) when needed.
- Create simple, independent and enjoyable settling tasks which incorporate choice.
- Find out the children's ideas and then use them.
- Discuss a clear pictorial timetable which highlights and smoothes lesson transitions – (see downloadable train timetable template, Resource 3.2).
- Get the children to help you organise and label your resources.
- Make sure everyone knows how to access and store resources independently.
- Keep the room looking attractive with tidy resources and interactive displays prepared with the children.
- Make sure everyone knows your expectations and values: have a go, try your best, it's okay to make mistakes – that's how we learn.

First	Then

Figure 3.1 A simple task sequence card

- Share some of yourself, your feelings and experiences with the children. Good teaching is built on the quality of teacher–pupil relationship.
- Celebrate and recognise achievement – have a wall of fame to daily display individual best work, and to welcome bright ideas.
- Create a space where children can go when they need time to chill and take control of their feelings.
- Regularly use class and group circle times supported by a worry box where they can express their feelings through posting their drawings or writing.
- Organise clear and achievable tasks; break instructions down into short clear sequences. Try an initial card simply drawn out with space for just two tasks (see Figure 3.1).
- Personalise these sequences into written or pictorial form beside the individual child.

All this time adds up to a highly organised learning area where each child is supported and included through an Emotionally Literate environment, an environment which both they and their peers have created and where everyone is both valued and respected. Often I hear teachers complain about the amount of time we spend on classroom discipline and redirection. The benefit to taking this time to prepare an Emotionally Literate environment is the independence and resilience of the children which it generates, allowing the teacher freedom to teach and the children freedom to learn. The EYFS Principle 1.4 states that *'Children gain a sense of well-being when they are encouraged to take responsibility and to join in by helping with manageable tasks that interest them'*. (DCSF, 2008)

How does Emotional Literacy Promote Positive Learning Behaviour?

In considering the tensions surrounding inclusion, Julie Allan (2003: 177) discusses the need to shift our thinking away from *'notions of including particular individuals or groups of children and towards constructing environments that include all children'*. We need to create an environment of emotional stability which can be an oasis in a young and turbulent life. Above all try to remember that it is most probably not the child's fault!

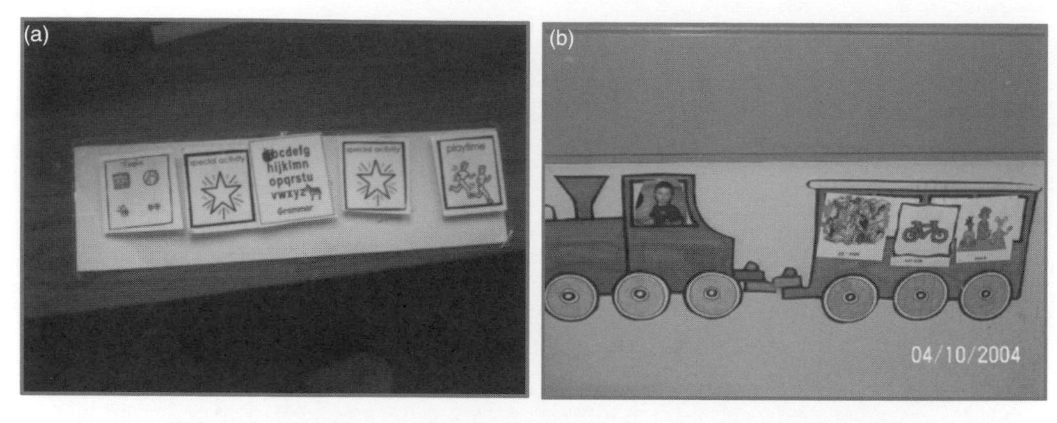

Photos 3.1 a and b Personalised short-term timetables. The star signifies free choice and this train has a photo of the child driving and has bike play as a personal choice.

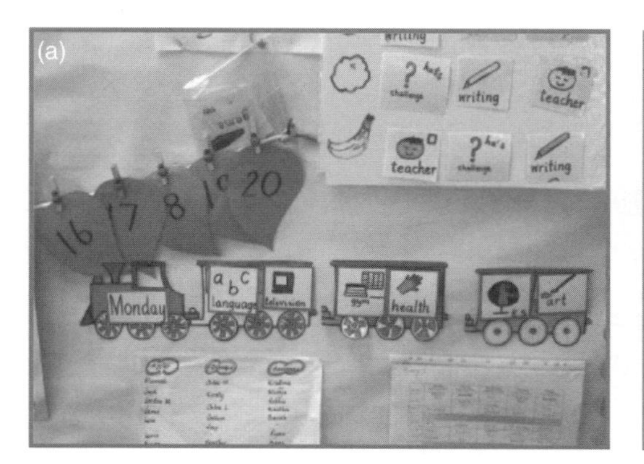

Photos 3.2 a and b Personalised daily timetables

Photo 3.3 Positive Behaviour Supports

Photos 3.4 a and b   Pictorial social stories

A Different Way to Form Groups

Once that supportive learning environment is created then consider how you will manage the inclusion and engagement of your pupils within it.

To Think About:

- *How does EL support growth of self esteem?*

Nursery Implementation (Age 3–5)

Through reflection on the initial project observations, discussed in Chapter 1, I decided to deviate from my usual practice of forming small groups based on stage and ability to concentrate, and to instead form groups based on observed skills in social interaction. Silveira et al. (1988) support this strategy, useful in empowering quiet withdrawn children to participate. This first initiative, based on a resource written by Bayley & Broadbent (2001), focused on Lola, a shy toy leopard cub, and supported the development of Emotional Literacy through communication skills. The planned activities encouraged group empathy, confidence and trust, through providing a safe opportunity for participation in repetitive language patterns modelled by staff. This built towards children being motivated and ready to learn.

To maintain her specialness Lola was kept in a decorative box specifically brought out for small group times. Nurturing routines were established with the children for getting her up and putting her to bed where each child greeted her or said good-bye in their own way, thus building important patterns of communication and interaction. The children seemed to establish a bond with Lola who like them was very young and unsure about the world. She needed their love and care. Some of this early work was videoed for later nursery team discussion. It was through this reflection on action that we decided, due to her popularity and success in bringing children together, that we should introduce three more soft toys as Lola's friends. This allowed each group to take responsibility for the care of their own 'pet', and so develop the notion of belonging. This solution proved very popular with both the children and the nursery adults.

The introductory work had observable benefits in developing confidence which the nursery team felt had encouraged the quieter children to participate in group activities. This established a basis for the work we then felt ready to start specifically on Emotional Literacy. Lola and her friends continued to visit group time during the nursery year and to take part in and support activities based on the resource, Baseline Communication and Language (Delamain & Spring, 2000), never losing popularity or the ability to support communication. The development of these interdisciplinary activities is discussed in Chapter 4.

Pre-Nursery Thoughts (Babies to Age 3)

The Nursery initiative described above could easily be adapted to support very young children through a soft toy kept in a special 'bed' and specifically brought out for transition times. A nurturing routine could be established for getting their pet up and putting it to bed, welcoming it or saying good-bye in their own way, so building important and personal patterns of communication and interaction.

Extension into Primary 1 (Age 5–6)

Making the transition from nursery into primary 1, the children were split into two classes and joined by new children from other neighbouring nurseries. We followed the research project children moving into primary 1a. These were the younger pupils and they made the transition along with myself, their nursery teacher. The notion of teacher-supported transition is a well established practice in our school, affording a high level of continuity for the children. The class now consisted of 19 continuing pupils from the two different morning and afternoon nursery sessions plus seven new pupils. Lola and her friends needed to stay in the nursery, however, reflecting on Lola's continuing popularity and initial ability to establish a bond, I introduced a toy kitten. Together we chose a name for her and effortlessly 'Rosie' filled Lola's shoes. Rosie supported the children in building familiarity with each other and their new situation. Through her I once again formed small groups based on social interaction rather than academic ability.

Reflecting on the transition and comparing it to my previous primary 1 experiences, I found the children to be more expressive, open and ready to take an active part in circle time activities. As they became more aware of Emotional Literacy their confidence grew in strength. The excerpt from my personal journal in Figure 3.2 reflects on a circle time game where the children must lie completely still to win.

> *I've never had a class who entered into the spirit of Sleeping Lions so well. Normally I would pick off one or more often several children at a time. Today they were so engrossed in the game that lots of them simply did not move! It was tempting just to leave them, but to their delight I declared them all winners. Quite an accomplishment for such little people!*
>
> [Game explained in Resource 4.7]

Figure 3.2 Personal journal extract, 26th August

The willing participation of so many children in activities had a positive effect for the additional children joining from other nurseries, giving the learning environment a feeling of warm caring and openness, an importance supported in Weare & Gray (2002). I added to this positive ethos by providing soft ephemeral music in the mornings and using essential oils to scent the room. The idea was that entering a peaceful, calm environment supported the smooth and relaxed transition from home to school and set the scene for classroom expectations. The calmness worked for most if not all children, with both parents and visiting students commenting on the warm, welcoming ambience of the room. I resolved to extend this idea into the start of each session, however the practicalities of remembering to switch on the music intervened. It was several weeks later while discussing classroom organisation with a colleague, before I thought of adding this as a responsibility for our band of classroom helpers.

Why is it Important for Children to Vocalise their Feelings?

The personal journal extract in Figure 3.3, demonstrates the quality of communication which Rosie the kitten was now supporting at these times. This was real, healthy discussion between the children, based on listening with constructive and empathetic response. It was not the usual primary 1 regurgitated 'news' while the rest of the class sat and fidgeted waiting for their shot. It demonstrates their growing awareness and identification of feelings.

It was during these morning inductions that time was taken to both talk to and listen to children as they settled into class, gathering together in our quiet area created for the purpose. Flexibility allowed the natural movement into daily tasks as we became ready. If on occasion this took longer than anticipated over the first few weeks this quickly sorted itself out as the children, confident in their new environment, quickly settled in and reaped the benefits of their positive start.

> *We discussed sad and lonely feelings today – It was introduced by I who as Rosie was passed round told us she didn't like her bedroom, she felt lonely and scared in it. She didn't like the dark. I asked the children for suggestions and they had lots of helpful advice from similar stories to real suggestions of getting out all your toys or teddies. B told us he liked to talk to his big bunny but when he told his Dad his Dad said that was a baby thing to do. B said he felt angry. G laughed he thought it was baby too, but J said he agreed it was unkind, he liked to talk to his elephant. This was such a mature, sensible discussion over problems very relevant to them. I felt privileged to be a part/included in their world!*

Figure 3.3 Personal journal extract, 8th September

The start of the week, particularly Monday morning, can often be an unsettled time as children need to reorganise their minds and sleep patterns to fit the school day. As a result of this project our whole school moved away from a Monday morning assembly to allow children personal and social development time in their own class groups. Generally this was a time for circle time activities and building on the above established routines. We started each circle time session with a whole-class circle but were then quite quickly able to split into four smaller circles based as before on social interaction. Expectations were set for engagement and were met with support from Rosie and her friends.

The use of small circles was highly popular and empowering for the children. As Hamill & Clark (2005) discuss, teacher attitudes and expectations communicate messages about ability and behaviour to the children Having spoken together in a large group, the children were now able to take this 'conversation' to their little group and make it their own. This allowed me the opportunity to sit for a few minutes with one group either to scaffold conversation or simply to quietly listen. If we were lucky enough to have support on occasion then the depth of the experience could be enhanced even more. The use of four small circles was easier for the children to manage, but if any child said something that required follow-up I could be free to support and facilitate this. Is it not the case that we underestimate the capabilities of our children?

Puppets and their Uses

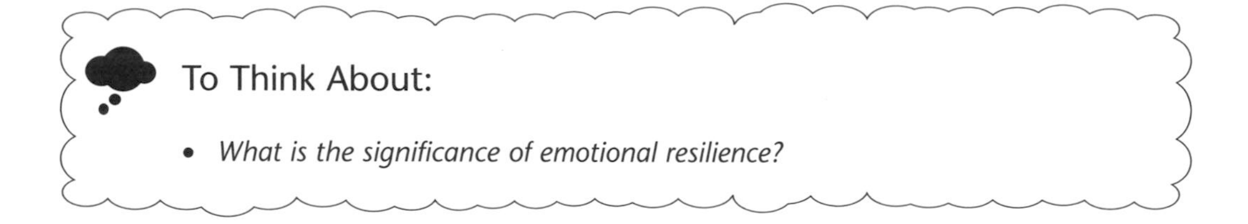

To Think About:

- *What is the significance of emotional resilience?*

Nursery Implementation (Age 3–5)

Reflecting on the formative assessment based on Clark (2001) being introduced throughout the school, I tried using glove puppets to introduce the learning intention or WALT (we are learning today) and success criteria or WILF (what I am looking for). Walt became a friendly green dragon and Wilf a cheeky wee boy. The fact that Wilf was a boy made him instantly more appealing to the boys and able to sit with the class group supporting and modelling good listening skills. I would not have believed how well those two puppets worked. They met other classes at assembly and visited nursery teachers' meetings as ambassadors to spread the word. The children often used the puppets in nursery to mimic my lessons and later they travelled with us into primary 1.

Considering the impact of Walt and Wilf and the quality of engagement they gave to learning, I purchased multicultural, child sized puppet buddies, which seemed perfect to extend this interest into Emotional Literacy within the pre-school transition project. Each day the puppets were introduced to the class with a little story

Photo 3.5 Thinking about the tadpoles

L was showing puppet Laura the tadpoles and quietly chatting to her. Quietly watching I could see that she was thinking, and then she asked with concern where the tadpoles' beds were? We then had a nice discussion re different animal homes. 'So... ' L. wanted to know, 'Where do the [puppet] buddies sleep?' A good question and one I hadn't thought of. We found a basket and a piece of cloth to make a blanket in the cupboard and made them a home this was a demonstration of real caring and concern for others.

Figure 3.4 Personal journal extract, 14th April on use of puppet as support for communication and learning

about how they were feeling that day. This was followed by a short discussion about how the children could welcome them into their play or help them cope with their day. This problem solving approach supported and developed emotional resilience and understanding. The children quickly and easily began to communicate through them and with them as Figure 3.4 demonstrates.

The Promoting Alternative Thinking Strategies or PATHS (Kusche & Greenberg, 1994) project supports this type of initiative. In PATHS turtle puppets are used to help children recognise their feelings and the expression 'doing turtle' is used to stop, take a deep breath and think before acting. Developing this idea with the children's favourite puppet called Gordon, we asked 'What would Gordon do?' And of course ... he would stop, take a deep breath and think! The children were learning to become more resilient through working with the puppets as intermediaries, developing respect and empathy while simultaneously they also supported class tasks such as emergent writing, communication and problem solving. I felt the puppets had added a new momentum to our development of emotional understanding and wanted to continue their use into primary 1, so with the children, together, we planned a puppet transition programme.

To Think About:

- *How do puppets support self esteem and growing Emotional Literacy?*

Extension into Primary 1 (Age 5–6)

The puppets shared their feelings of excitement and apprehension with the nursery children about moving to 'the big school' and made short introductory visits with little groups to research their many questions. 'What do you need to take?' 'Do you get a snack?' 'Where do you play?' 'Where do I put my things?' 'What happens at lunch time?' Each time on returning from a fact-finding mission the puppets supported the children in reporting back and showing an object to add to our nursery school play area, for example, a lunch box or photo.

During the transition to primary 1, at the children's request, the puppets moved by basket into their new home. They then had to learn new rules just like the children and find their way around the big school. Each day, unlike nursery, only one buddy came out and extended their story before choosing to spend their day with one 'special' child who was responsible for their care. This worked very well as a support to enhancing confidence and positive behaviour strategies as the two examples in Figure 3.5 illustrate.

Extension into Primary 2, Primary 3 and Beyond (Age 6–8+)

Using the puppets as intermediaries in this way changed my approach and created new opportunities to develop pupil emotional resilience and problem solving. Reflecting

*C ate her packed lunch at playtime on her first full day at school. Puppet Nicola was '**worried**' about her doing it again and was able to reassure her by spending the day in C's care.*

E was observed over three consecutive days punching the puppets. Despite discussion and unhappy face warning cards being given this behaviour seemed to be escalating. Perhaps E was looking for more attention. I asked his Mum in for a chat and we sat down together with E to discuss and agree acceptable behaviour. It was agreed E had been unkind and together we discussed when these things happened and how we could help him control his behaviour. We decided together that it was often when he didn't have enough space or wanted to play. So E agreed to try sitting in a seat with more space, using a cushion which defined his personal space while on the carpet and getting Gordon the puppet to help him. It is worth noting E was one of the 7 new children.

Figure 3.5 Puppet support

Photo 3.6 The puppet buddies' home in P1

on the success of this approach I made a request to the Parents Association for funding to purchase a large puppet to be taken care of by each of the infant classes.

The puppets arrived and for each a letter was written introducing them to the class as a new pupil. We put the puppets in boxes ready for delivery then a support assistant knocked on individual class doors at a prearranged delivery time. At this point as each class took individual ownership, each class teacher wrote their puppet a little potted history.

Puppets have an unnerving way of ingratiating themselves and soon our new puppets became involved in development scenarios across the curriculum. Puppet school bags were bought, reading books given out, puppet coat pegs and personal drawers labelled. The puppets were introduced to the school community and taken to assembly. Staff became inspired as they chatted and collaborated using photographs to develop personal and social development (PSD) and problem solving.

The puppets experienced the full range of emotions as the following year they moved up a stage with their classes. In primary 3 and 4 they started visiting homes for sleepovers, received party invitations to other classes, letters of thanks and birthday cards. Children designed and made puppet costumes for the Halloween party. They supported Enterprise Education in fundraising and collected paper for the Eco school project. They became the school puppet family, for example Sally Puppet in 3a had a younger sister, Emma, who was anxious about starting school, while Sandeep, her cousin and best friend in 3b, was being bullied. The possibilities for developing emotional resilience are endless. Children took photos and used them in word documents to form a book for the front reception area of the school, where parents and visitors could read about our puppet exploits. Always the puppets added to our growing awareness of Emotional Literacy. They could empathise with children, enhance learning intentions and encourage positive behaviour and resilience, supporting inclusion in so many ways.

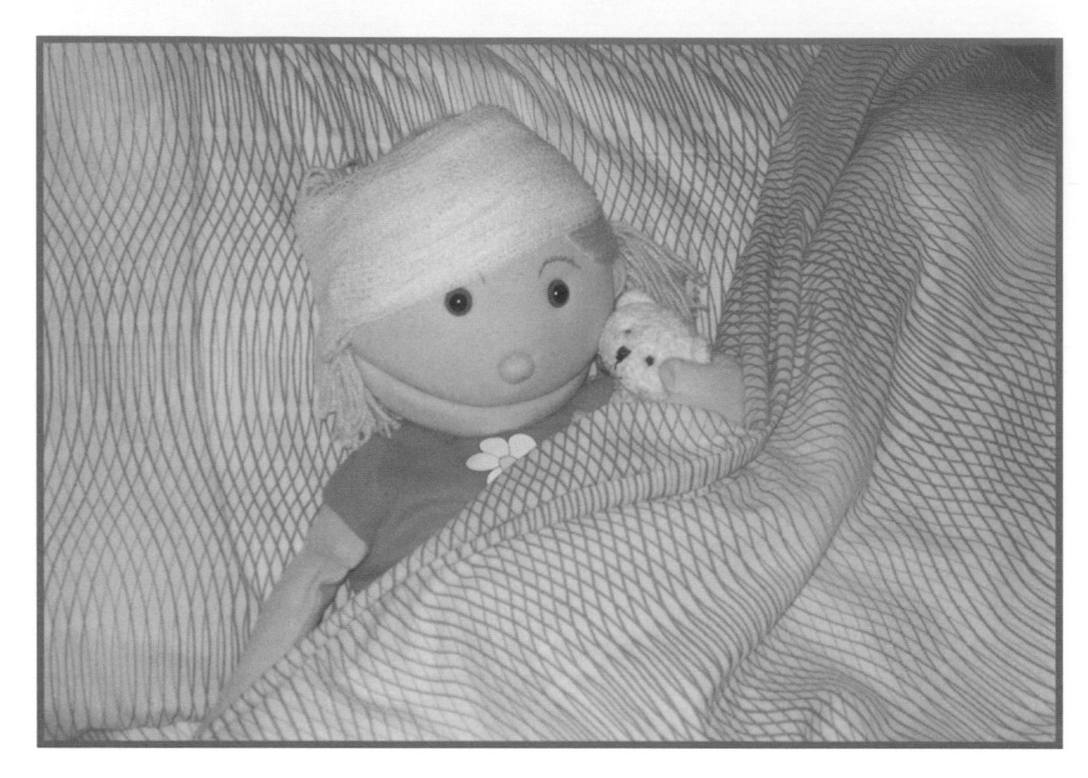

Photo 3.7 Laura Puppet's Mum sent in a letter to explain her absence from school

Photo 3.8 Friends: Laura and her cousin Sandeep Puppet play in the park after school

Photo 3.9 Laura was proud of her writing today

Photo 3.10 Laura phoned her Mum to ask if she could stay at her friend's house for tea

Building Self Esteem

A child's self esteem is their personal evaluation of themselves. This is the difference between their self image and their ideal self. Children build up a self concept from their impression of the way others respond to them. An ideal image is a comparison to the images modelled around them. Children with low self esteem find it difficult to participate in lessons since they worry they will fail. As stated earlier, a child with sound self esteem is more resilient when challenged by new learning experiences (Morris, 2002; Colwell & Hammersley-Fletcher, 2004), while the troubled child, having used their emotional energy in coping with personal problems, can become quickly frustrated. This then has a huge impact over times of transition when resilient children demonstrate their greater capability to settle to learning. Children who are challenged by barriers to inclusion can be supported and empowered through a school community which works together to generate an ethos of inclusion, as Barnes (2005) supports, an inclusive learning environment where their voice is valued. Perhaps most of all this would be a community where children have the social and emotional skills and resilience to look out for each other. In our school the puppet buddies now support our children in learning these skills. The EYFS Principle 1.4 states that *'Making friends and getting on with others helps children to feel positive about themselves and others'.* (DCSF, 2008) Also Frederickson & Cline (2009) acknowledge the strength of peer reinforcement as one of the strongest motivators for learning.

Teachers are an important part of this learning environment and can become attachment figures for children, acting as powerful role models. In an emotionally literate, inclusive environment they can express care and demonstrate the importance they place in valuing children as they are, thereby developing the child's sense of self. Within that environment teachers can raise self esteem simply through developing their relationship with pupils, and employing firm, fair boundaries which give their pupils a genuine voice in decision-making and teach responsibility to oneself and each other. If we listen to our children and understand the need to look deeper, beyond their masks, we avoid emotional misunderstandings. We can then work to improve self esteem, behaviour and learning motivation of the individual child.

A commitment to an Emotionally Literate approach to inclusion is an ongoing daily process which develops a sense of belonging, self esteem and the skills to develop resilience and responsibility. Inclusion starts with us and how we see it. Working on the premise that bad behaviour is usually intended to meet a legitimate need; it is the strategies used that can be at fault. Emotional Literacy can develop a greater sense of perspective through learning empathy and tolerance of difference in others. It increases our ability to communicate with and relate to different types of people, creating a sense of belonging which Morris (2002) supports, and which Faupel (2002) claims to be the most effective way to establish and maintain an inclusive community for everyone. Evans & Lunt (2002: 3) point out that inclusive education is about values and principles, *'about the kind of society that we want and the kind of education that we value'.* Then they ask in the current educational climate, what do the policy makers and practitioners assess as the limits to inclusive education?

> Social and emotional skills are a key component of an emotionally healthy, inclusive school culture that helps all pupils succeed and which values and celebrates diversity. (DCSF, 2005)

To Think About:

- *What elements of my practice can I change to become more inclusive?*
- *How do you measure effective inclusion?*

Further Reading

Bayley, R. & Broadbent, L. (2001) *Supporting the Development of Listening, Attention and Concentration Skills: Helping Young Children to Listen.* This is a delightful resource and is also very useful in developing belonging with nursery aged children.

Delamain, C. & Spring, J. (2000) *Developing Baseline Communication Skills.* This is a very useful resource bank of games and activities to support skills across the literacies.

Hamill, P. & Clark, K. (2005) *Additional Support Needs* has good examples of individual learning plans. For pre-school see Chapter 5, and for primary see Chapter 6.

Topping, K. & Maloney, S. (eds) (2005) *The Routledge Falmer Reader in Inclusive Education.* Oxford: Routledge.

Whitehead, J. (2007) 'Telling it Like It Is: Developing Social Stories for Children in Mainstream Primary Schools', *Pastoral Care in Education,* 25 (4): 35–41.

This is a link to the PATHS website which has a multitude of papers and other information regarding the intervention: www.prevention.psu.edu/projects/PATHSPublications.html

Electronic Resources

Go to www.sagepub.co.uk/chirstinebruce for electronic resources for this chapter:

3.1 A Checklist for Emotional Inclusion

3.2 Individualised Train Timetable Template

3.3 Positive Behaviour Support Cards

3.4 Puppet Letter

Using Emotional Literacy Across the Curriculum

In this chapter, I consider:

- **The activities that were part of our Emotional Literacy project**
- **How these activities came about and how they were extended across the transition from pre-school into the first school year, and in many cases beyond.**

Classroom Initiatives

The flexibility of the action research process came into its own as the project evolved through reflection on action. I found my research journey was non-linear with activities springing up in different activity and curricular areas. These initiatives were supported through professional reading and included a series of in-service opportunities, pupil observations, journal reflections, group activity evaluations and collegiate discussion. I have provided a reflective narrative of the journey below which employs the Altrichter et al. (1993) model of the action research process. This requires finding a starting point, then clarifying the situation, through observation, reflection and planning in order to develop action strategies in a continuous cycle which includes sharing and discussing knowledge gained with colleagues. The initiatives which evolved as the result of this action research cycle were not neat and tidy in a uniform spiral of action research cycles, but often simultaneous, overlapping and at times disjointed.

Circle Time as an Approach

As already discussed, the most effective teaching and learning takes place within an effective teacher–pupil relationship, where children feel safe, motivated, actively involved and participate in a range of positive learning opportunities. The underlying principles of circle time (Mosley, 1996) lend themselves to establishing feelings of belonging, supporting both inclusion and skills in communication, and so is an important component of the Emotional Literacy approach. It is worth taking the time to establish effective circle time procedures as a prerequisite to developing skills in Emotional Literacy. Some excellent books are listed in the further reading section of this chapter, however there are one or two points worth making here.

- It is vital to take time from the start to get the circle right so that it is totally inclusive, nobody is squashed out and each child can see every other child.
- To create a safe, supportive and encouraging environment it is important to establish ground rules with the children for acceptable behaviour. They must listen to others and respect their rights and opinions. There can be no 'put downs' only a constructive exchange of ideas with an option to 'pass' without embarrassment.
- It is worth starting and finishing with a 'fun' activity so that everyone feels happy, safe and confident.
- The circle should empower the children to participate with confidence, independence and ownership of their circle.

Just as children themselves are each unique, so are the needs, concerns and problems they carry with them. Some children will arrive at school unable to start learning until these are recognised. The issues should be quietly talked through with support in identifying their available choices and then in selecting preferable actions. While some of their concerns may be easily rectified within class, there will be times when a more sensitive issue brought up during the circle needs further individual exploration. In these circumstances it is important to have a system in place whereby you can contact a member of the management team to provide time in a more private environment. This aspect is revisited in Chapter 5 (see page 79), however often the most effective strategy within the pupil–teacher relationship is for the teacher simply to provide a listening ear.

Communication Skills

The ability to communicate our thoughts and feelings is of central importance to Emotional Literacy as was discussed in earlier chapters. A useful resource to develop these skills is *Developing Baseline Communication Skills* by Delamain & Spring (2000). This resource book became the backbone of the intervention, for which we built our own custom-made planning and evaluation pro-forma. These evaluations informed changes to our planning and practice on a day-to-day basis and built a personalised bank of ready planned activities specific to our needs. Pitched at an appropriate level for the age group, *Developing Baseline Communication Skills* is of particular interest due to its breadth across the curriculum while acknowledging the importance of basic skills. It also provides ideas to build self esteem and social emotional skills, encourages child–child talk and considers diversity of individual development.

Nursery Implementation (Age 3–5)

Historically we have not used the key worker system in our nursery, however now building on our earlier findings we organised our groups so that each member of

> *We each take our own 'key' group through a rotation of 4 activities. Today I took a double group which allowed 'S' to take the time to observe 'C' leading and supporting the activity she is due to do tomorrow. S was then able to discuss what had worked well and how it might work best for her own group. While C could add what had worked well for her and why she had chosen that approach.*

Figure 4.1 Personal journal extract, from 25th April

staff retained a 'key' group for 1 term, building a sense of belonging. Termly rotation then allowed individual children to experience the strengths of each staff member while evaluations gave an excellent opportunity for triangulation of data. Recorded daily, the data highlighted children with extra needs in learning or behaviour. Each member of staff was also able to improve their own practice and the overall ability of the team through the daily sharing of evaluations of practice. The flexibility to adapt and develop differentiated activities and learning themes increased our child-centred approach. Short sections captured on video along with journal reflections like the example in Figure 4.1 were used to demonstrate our progress and to support and improve our practice.

Extension into Primary 1 (Age 5–6)

We continued to use activities from *Developing Baseline Communication Skills* revising and reinforcing some well known games before moving on to new activities.

Findings

Naturally as the children entered their first school year there were changes to staff ratios and a whole-class approach was required, however this caused less of a problem than I had anticipated. The possible reasons for this may well be that:

- Most of the children were familiar with the circle-time routine
- We were revisiting games familiar to many of the class
- The children were more mature
- Pupils and staff had different expectations of primary 1
- The children may have had a strongly developed feeling of self esteem.

Although all the children took part, when reflecting on our progress I had a few concerns about individual pupils (see Figure 4.2). In all these incidences contact was maintained with the family. The arrival of a nursery nurse student allowed me to address these problems through the reintroduction of a group for quiet, withdrawn children (see Chapter 3, page 35) where, within the support of the small group, these problems were aired and worked through on two sessions per week. This was an idea based on the nurture group approach as discussed earlier in Chapter 2 (see page 24) (Bennathan & Boxall, 1996; Savage, 2001).

> *Pupil H hadn't told me he was worried about coming to school leaving his Mum to explain for him. I had already discussed our concerns about his readiness for school with his parents.*
>
> *G was fretful but she couldn't explain why, possibly she was still learning to cope with the arrival of her new sibling.*
>
> *J had regressed to a much quieter and indeed stubborn child since starting school. When I spoke to Mum it transpired she had planned a return to work coinciding with his first weeks at school.*

Figure 4.2

> *B – I'm a number 4 cause I'd rather be at my Gran's.*
>
> *E – 2 'cause I've not had any breakfast. Mummy had no milk.*

Figure 4.3 Extract from my journal, 1st November

While mulling over these problems a snippet read in *TES* triggered thoughts of solution-focused theory and during the next few sessions we started to use this approach, the children deciding how they were feeling on a scale of 1–10. This has been an excellent initiative for monitoring confidence to express feelings and opinions, as Figure 4.3 demonstrates, and met the planned project objectives. Again the ability of the children to give a reasoned explanation for their choice of level surprised and delighted me, their understanding of this quite mature concept demonstrating a developing sense of self awareness. I wondered if this was further evidence of the progress we had achieved. In fact this extended activity was shared with my colleagues and has been adopted by the rest of the school. You may find the activity sheet provided in Resource 2.4 useful.

Story and Drama

Like most early years practitioners I believe that stories are an intrinsic part of early years education and a strong teaching medium. The following initiative emerged as a result of reflection on the problem of how to modify and channel the energy from rowdy 'cartoon character' based play of a group of predominantly pre-school boys. As is so often the case the play started imaginatively but rapidly lost structure becoming wild and out of control. This group behaviour is displayed annually across nurseries and while it is important to recognise the need to play out different emotions, for example fear or death, in a safe environment, it can be argued from a social constructivist view that play needs adult guidance to move forward.

Nursery Implementation (Age 3–5)

Although many participative stories were shared with the children, 'The Three Billy Goats Gruff' was a recurring favourite and one of our greatest successes. This traditional story, full of pace and dynamic expression lends itself to dramatisation with the addition of percussion sound effects as each little goat anxiously 'trip traps' over the bridge under which the angry troll lives. The children quickly became totally immersed in building up the story in their role play around the nursery and I grasped the opportunity to capture their facial expressions through photograph's for later use. We also observed the group play which resulted after children had chosen to use the listening centre to re-listen to the story. This version of the story, set against atmospheric music, led the group into spontaneous dramatisation freely flowing to the nearby climbing frame. Over the weeks as other stories were told and acted out, groups of children kept returning to this as their best loved story. It is interesting to note that these impromptu dramatisations generally took place outwith the role play area, taking place instead in the large block play area, or with the climbing apparatus. Perhaps the children were making a group statement that this was not simple 'house' play but something more important and adventurous. The structure of this story set realistic boundaries yet encouraged ownership and creativity through extended imaginative play. It supported pupil skills in collaborative communication, thus allowing expressive language to become embedded in social interaction and conflict resolution to be fully explored in a safe context. Although this dramatic play did succeed in channelling their energy and moving the children on from simple rough and tumble play to a more sophisticated use of language and greater quality and depth of interaction, it did not stop rowdy play completely, but simply gave it a structure which allowed the children to develop resilience and the means of learning self control.

Photo 4.1 'Please, don't eat me up' said the middle Billy Goat Gruff, 'my big brother is much more tasty'

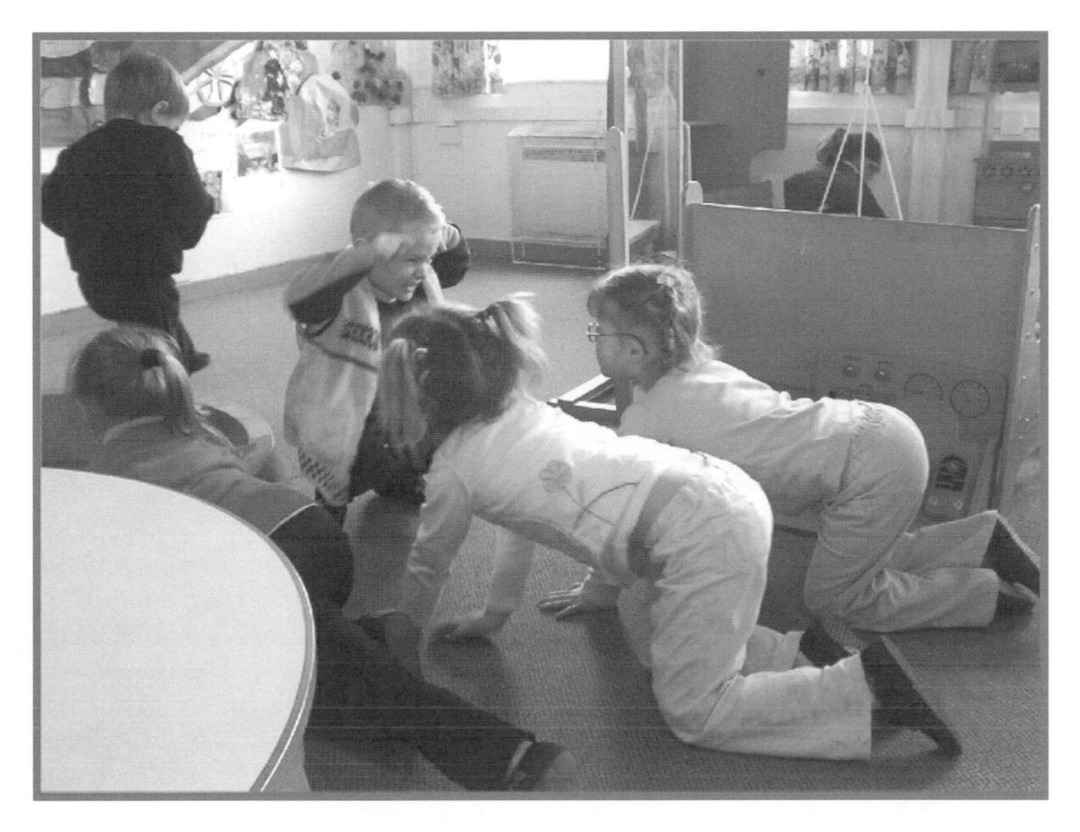

Photo 4.2 'Right', said the biggest Billy Goat Gruff to the other two Billy Goats Gruff, 'listen carefully, this is the plan ...'

Photos 4.3 a and b Photographic observations of the 'minimalist' role play resources provided in primary 1 which encouraged creative and free flowing play

Extension into Primary 1 (Age: 5–6)

While working within the confines of a classroom timetable, I wished to support and extend the possibilities for 'story and drama' play in the first school year. The positive impact of encouraging play is endorsed in the work of Ahn (2005) and Bergen (2002) who found pretend play allowed the development of social and linguistic skills. Reflecting on the nursery dramatic play, which often occurred out with the designated drama area and with minimal props, I decided to try simplifying the resources I provided; support for this can be found in Bilton (2002). I left only a box of miscellaneous hats and several simple cardboard boxes in the role play area, the 'house' then became an area of continual redesign and rebuilding within each school day, resourced by the children themselves as they took on new roles. This was supported through report-back sessions by the children, where children were encouraged to express their own views, feelings and ideas to the rest of the class. The resulting dramatic play was kept fresh and exciting as storylines flowed from one story to another building again on expressive vocabulary and communication. A difference had also been noted by myself and by other staff in the ability of the children to participate freely, sensibly and imaginatively in timetabled drama lessons in the hall.

Further Extension beyond the First Year (Age 7–8)

I believe there is a place for this kind of play throughout school as a basis for developing and extending literacy and for creative writing in particular. In many schools, space to set up specific areas can become a real challenge so I have a couple of suggestions. First, if we are talking 'minimalist' here, then a large cardboard box decorated by the children themselves to make a dressing up box can work wonders, particularly if a letter goes home asking for parental support in collecting suitable items. Another perhaps lower key and more manageable solution is to make more use of small world play as children grow older. Story lines can be first built and vocalised during play with the potential of using animation to support and extend the written word. Personally I have both role play and small world play running alongside each other. It is important to give small world play its own space so that play can be developed and not always tidied away.

Using Photography

Nursery Implementation (Age 3–5)

The impromptu photographs of expression taken while the children were absorbed in story play were exciting and I reflected on how best to use them to extend emotional learning. Enlarged and laminated, I introduced the photographs as part of an interactive display around a mirror where they became an indispensable resource for discussion between staff, pupils, parents, visitors and combinations of all of these (see Photo 2.3 on page 19). Originally a spontaneous activity, supported by McMinn (2003), this became the new focus of the project. As the collection of photographs mounted around the mirror grew, children enjoyed sitting on the nursery rocking chair and copying the expressive faces for each other. As our collection of expression photographs spread around the nursery, supporting the understanding of Emotional Literacy, we observed parents on many occasions discussing them with their children. It is interesting that the SEAL projects now produces a pack of similar emotion postcards, which I found particularly useful when extending my work into primary 3 and 4. However, there is nothing which can replace the power of using the children's own images.

Photo 4.4 is a snapshot of a pre-school pupil discussing our transition display with her father. The display showed photos of all the pre-school children blasting off to their new schools and the rockets would go with the children to be displayed in

Photo 4.4 Developing a sense of Emotional Literacy. A pupil talking to her Daddy about how her friends in the photographs are feeling

their new classes. The observed conversation was of interest since the pupil was not talking about her own feelings, but those of her peers who were 'feeling anxious and excited too' about going to their new schools. The child was explaining how individual children were feeling and why. Through this she was able to raise her family's awareness of the mixture of emotions she might be experiencing herself.

Discussion of the emotion and anxieties around transition was found to be a support to transition by Brown & Dunn (1996) and Barlow & Stewart Brown (2001) who found that parents valued the opportunity to think through emotions and empathise with their children.

Extension into Primary 1 (Age 5–6)

Reflecting on the success of the expression photographs as a support to communication in the nursery setting, I planned to re-use the mirror idea for pupils entering

B explained; 'I've an uncomfortable feeling about falling out with my Nan, but you see I'm bored of going to her house'.

Figure 4.4 Personal journal extract, 3rd October

C's Mum: 'You know we're moving house next week right? Well you could have heard my jaw drop when C came out and said he was feeling apprehensive about it. I was amazed and he used it in the right context too'.

Figure 4.5 Personal journal extract

primary 1 and extend this to support problem resolution by adding caption bubbles with the children. Their memories of the actual nursery events were outstanding, the photographs initiating extended discussion between the children about past events, and it did not take much teacher direction to relate them to the present. They could remember clearly not only the incidents but also the events which had led up to them, proving that the impact of the use of their own images was obviously substantial; Photo 2.4 (page 19) shows the ensuing display. I continued to develop this idea allowing the children, with a little support, to take their own photographs, then together we made up a class PowerPoint slide show for their parents' open evening. This was a highly successful activity which developed feelings of class inclusion and belonging.

Reflecting on what we had achieved, I realised the children must have improved their understanding of expression and in considering where to go next I asked the class to sort the photographs into 'comfortable' and 'uncomfortable' feelings (Kelly et al., 2004). I was delighted to find the children could do this with ease and could also explain why they had sorted them that way. I then extended this through a similar exercise using commercially printed drawings. This activity proved more of a challenge for the children but sparked confident discussion over issues such as where 'surprise' fitted in 'because you get nice surprises and nasty ones'. I thought the introduction of the written vocabulary would be too difficult but, reassured during collegiate discussion, I decided to give it a try. Children do take pleasure from using impressive vocabulary, as Figures 4.4 and 4.5 support and they certainly took delight in recognising some of the written expressions.

Again, after some thought I developed this further by putting the pictures into uncomfortable and comfortable bags for a circle time activity. Choosing a card from the bag, children recounted a past experience 'I feel .... when ....' First we had the bag for comfortable feelings only, then the uncomfortable feelings bag only, then finally the choice of both bags. Rosie the kitten was passed around the circle to a familiar rhyme to support random turn taking and I kept the number of turns down to 10, pre-empting any restlessness. It is interesting to note that 9 out of 10 children chose from the uncomfortable bag, presumably enjoying the opportunity to talk about an unpleasant feeling. Some children liked to look and choose specific feelings to tell a particular story.

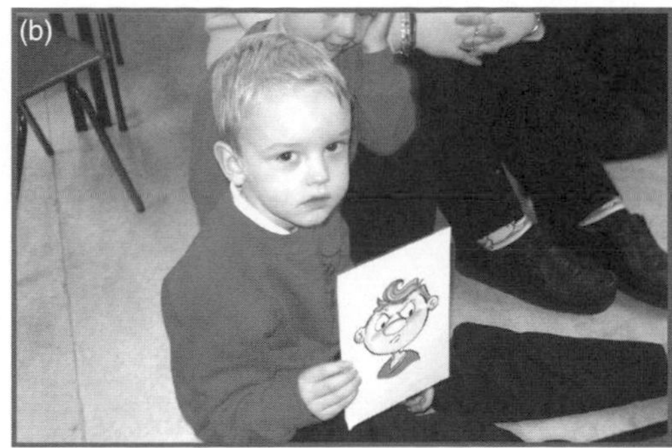

Photos 4.5 a and b Most children chose to talk about a time when they experienced an uncomfortable feeling

The activity promoted a development using the big book *The Huge Bag of Worries* by Virginia Ironside (see Photo 4.6) before returning full circle to the Baseline Communication activity 'Worry Beads'. In this activity the children thread a bead as they share their worry, again an appropriate and popular activity where the children supported one another (see Resource 4.7). This activity was in turn shared with colleagues following the action research cycle and used throughout the school.

The primary 1 classroom, unlike our nursery, had internet connection and made it possible to use the BBC website, CBeebies Emotion Theatre on the smart board and individual i-books. I found the programme characters and web games worked particularly well, their familiarity forming a link between home and school, which was picked up and extended by some pupils and their families at home.

Extension Ideas beyond Primary 1 (Age 7–8)

Games and stories which encourage discussion of feelings and emotions are appropriate at any stage. The discussion evoked is important to our mental health and wellbeing and also supports the trusting partnership we need to build with our pupils. It is unusual for a story not to incorporate some emotional expression and once you start thinking with an Emotionally Literate mind, you will find that your favourite stories can quite easily be used to support activities which build empathy and resilience.

Extension Activities

Activity 1: Paper Chain People

'We are each unique and can feel different.' In this activity each child designs and makes a symmetrical double-faced collage person with outstretched arms. The person should be large enough to hold an A4 caption card. They are then allocated a letter from the alphabet and asked to create a comfortable facial expression to match the letter on one side, adding an appropriate caption card, then the opposite uncomfortable emotional expression on the other side. The children can use 'word art' to make their caption cards then present them at assembly. They can explain their understandings of how each of us is unique and can feel different; how each of us needs support to cope with our feelings, yet that each of us is still included and belongs. The letters could be used to spell out words such as resilience, empathy and Emotional Literacy.

Photo 4.6 Our big bag of worries

Photo 4.7 Threading our worries

Photo 4.8 An alphabet of emotions

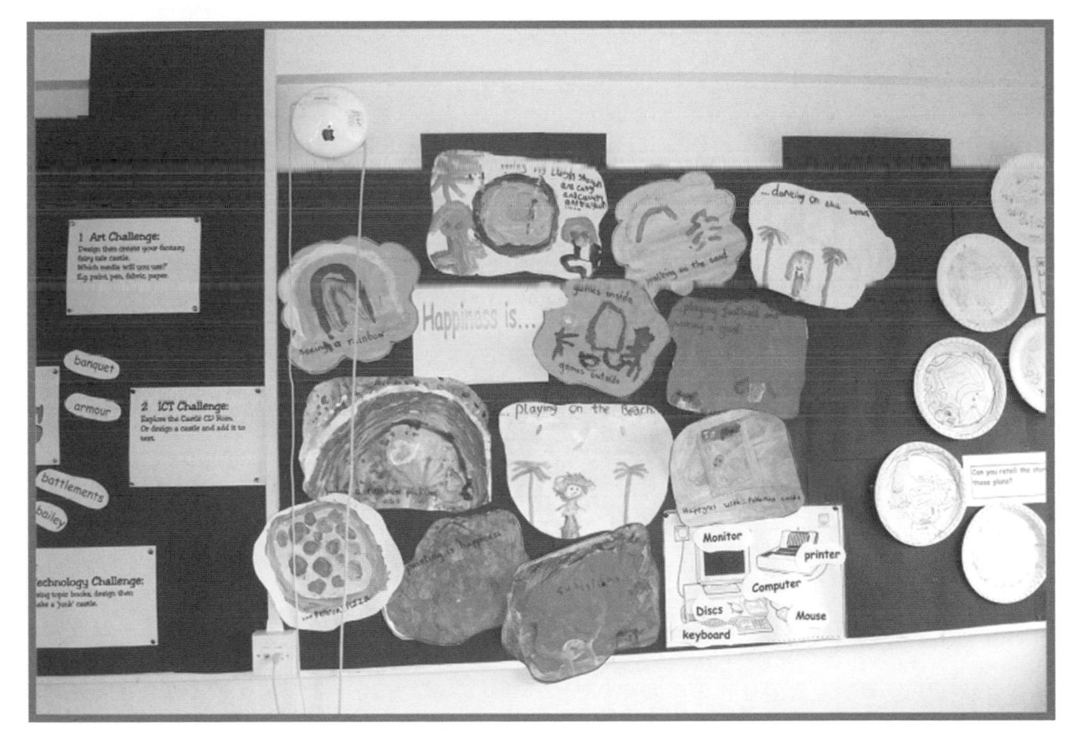

Photo 4.9 Happiness is ...

Activity 2: Visualisation

'We can relax through visualisation.' Make sure the children are sitting comfortably in their own space. Ask them to close their eyes and breath in deeply and quietly

(a)

(b)

Photos 4.10 a and b Anger and serenity

through their nose and exhale gently through their mouths. I usually ask them to think of each part of their body in turn from their toes to their heads to tense the muscles in that body part then relax. Once calm, ask them to think of a time when they felt really blissfully happy. Ask them to visualise it. What does it feel like? Smell, taste, sound like? Ask them to share their memory with their learning buddy or in a small circle of four or five children. Give the children the opportunity to use paint to record their memory, considering the best colours to express how they felt. Ask them to explain why they felt so happy and what it felt like inside. You will be

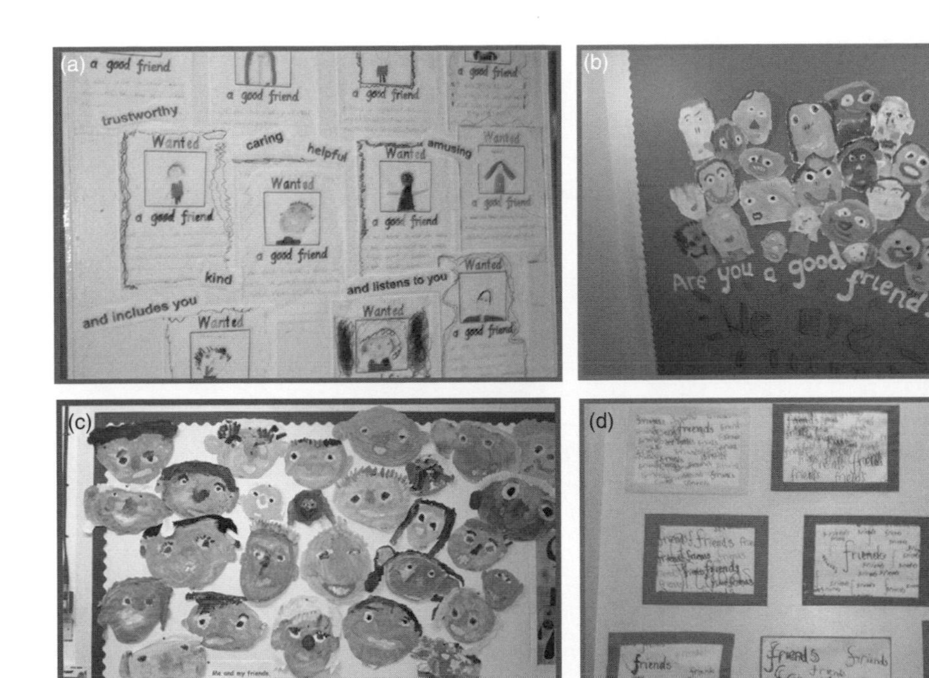

Photos 4.11 a, b, c and d Developing friendship skills (a) Wanted posters for a good friend (b) and (c) Self portraits, What does a good friend look like? (d) A colourful friendship handwriting activity

starting to teach them the skill of finding inner peace. This is a fantastic starting point for creative writing activities.

Activity 3: Graffiti

'We can each choose our words and actions.' You may feel this activity is 'risqué', however I found it very useful in bonding with some children with particular emotional difficulties. Start through discussing anger. Ask what makes them or others angry. Discuss how it makes them feel considering each of the senses in turn. Ask them what colour they think anger is, which words express anger and what they do when they are angry. Consider what makes some words angry and why we use them; what is allowed or forbidden and why. Usually it is the manner in which words are used rather than the words themselves. Now tell the children they are going to make a collaborative frieze called anger. Ask them to take a black felt pen and write angry graffiti on A5 paper – give them the freedom to write anything they like then to use colour to add dynamics to their work. Some children may need to be convinced that they are in a 'safe' environment to use the words while others will revel in the freedom. The result is exhilarating, enlightening and therapeutic. You might want to play background music such as 'Mars' from *The Planet* Suite by Holst. Once Anger is completed the following lessons should be devoted to Peace and Serenity in a similar fashion, this time the background music might be 'Prélude à l'après-midi d'un faune' by Debussy. There was a great deal of parental interest in this work, children talked about it at home, and what it meant to them. When the parents came in to see it at our open evening they thought it had been a particularly worthwhile activity which had developed their children's understanding.

Photos 4.12 a, b and c Puppets developing care, confidence and belonging with 8-year-olds (a) Enjoying a bus ride (b) In a castle dungeon (c) Confidence in independent reading

Activity 4: Friendship

'I know how to be a good friend.' As previously stated children copy the behaviour they see modelled around them. In trying to determine what a good friend consists of they need to consider their own social interactions with others. As Sheppy (2009) explains, children often initially build on the relationships they have observed in the family. Learning about friendship includes learning to empathise with the feelings, views and ideas of others. I think it is quite possible then to describe true friendship as an opposite to bullying. In developing the skills to be a good friend you might be considered to simultaneously be opening the subject of what a bully is and what a good friend can do to provide support in this situation.

Discuss what a good friend is like. Consider their expression, attitude, voice and personality. Ask the children how they would know when they have a good friend. If you were advertising for a good friend what qualities would you look for? Ask the children to make a 'Wanted' poster for a friend; there is an example in Resource 4.3 (see also Photo 4.11a). Discuss and act out how they would manage tricky situations when things go wrong. Make a little box of scenario cards for free role play. This is all part of developing skills in resilience. Ask them what a good friend would do if they saw you being bullied. Here is an opportunity for some more role play cards.

Photo 4.13 Energetic nursery parachute activities

Photo 4.14 Developing a sense of belonging

> *I asked the class what they'd like to do for Golden Time to celebrate their hard work this week.*
> *CR asked: 'Can we have bare feet with the parachute again? 'Yes, yes' the class all said, this would be what they wanted!*

Figure 4.6 Personal journal entry, 16th September, discussing golden time

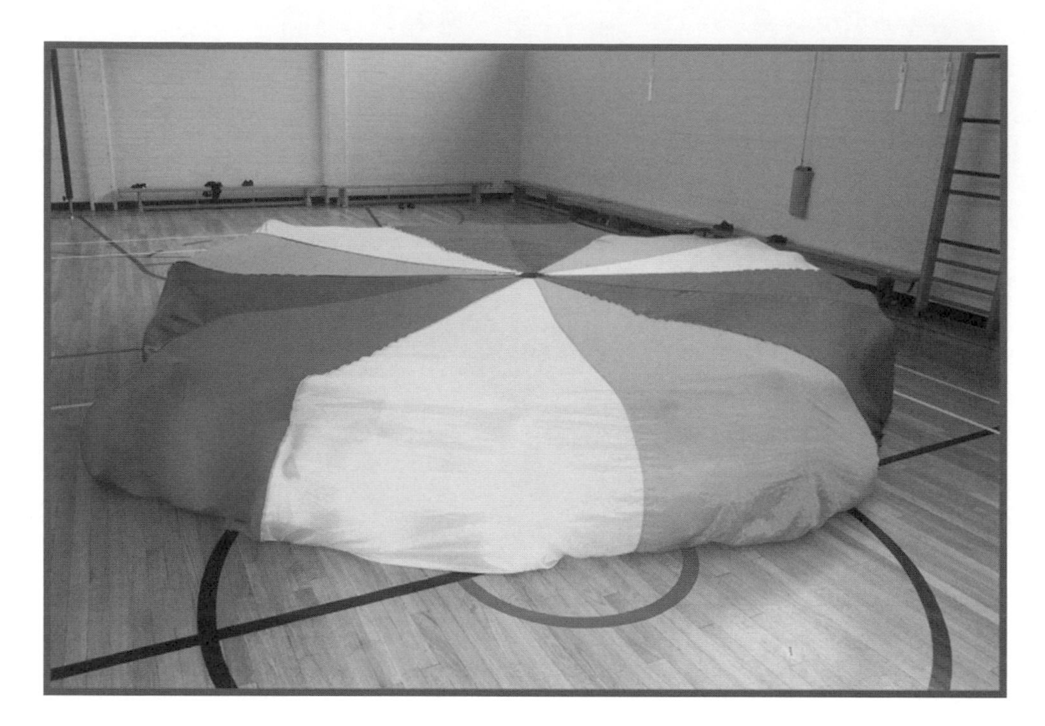

Photo 4.15 An independent parachute dome

Photo 4.16 Parachute fun outdoors

The children wanted to make a dome or tent and organised their own singing – I was outside taking the photo! A real sense of fun and belonging – a family! Togetherness! I felt proud!!

Figure 4.7 Personal journal entry, 30th September

Photo 4.17 Communication and negotiation out of doors

Parachute Activities

Nursery Implementation (Age 3–5)

Our early attempts at parachute activities were supported through Lola our toy leopard cub, who was introduced in Chapter 3. Initially we used semi-transparent fabric as our parachute with a small group, one child lay underneath while the rest of the group raised and lowered the fabric overhead and sang a chosen nursery rhyme. Support for this type of activity being linked to emotional development can be found in Bilton (2002: 111) and also Leavitt et al. (2003). Later in the year, wanting to build on the activity while keeping the security of the small group, a proper small-group parachute was purchased by the school. We felt it was important for the staff to take turns in lying underneath modelling, but also allowing an opportunity to extend independent group cooperation. This work was very successful in developing a sense of belonging, trust and confidence.

The parachute activities were extended into using the large parachute both in the school gym and outdoors with small groups of children underneath and opportunities to explore play in bare feet. Each new experience, built on reflection on action, added a new element of learning and excitement. Manipulating either the small or large parachute required cooperation, problem solving and team work.

Area: Garden **Context:** Hoop targets – bean bag throwing

CL, HL, C and A: The 4 children are at the bean bags and hoops activity. CL is organising the game. There is discussion about scores for reaching the different hoops. He has excellent aim and tries it out, scoring highly. The other children call out random scores and you can see the pride in his posture. The children then negotiate where the hoops should be put and where the cones that they should stand and throw from should be for the next round. CL praises A and C for their efforts then for his own turn he moves the hoops further away to make it harder for himself. The others watch and tell him 'you're doing well, well done'. The children are all supportive and encourage each other to aim carefully. The game dissolves as the children move on to the big ball & cones.

Figure 4.8 Developing skills in communication and negotiation

Area: Garden **Context**: Soft inflatable ball

B & J are standing at opposite sides of the ball which is hanging on a rope from the tree. They are taking turns at punching while the other holds the ball. There is lots of laughter. B comes over and hovers watching, then takes an opportunity for a shot. She is quickly told to 'get in the queue, then you can go next.'
B: 'This is good. I feel brave. I'm strong'.
J: 'Yeah, I feel powerful.'
B: 'Hey look at us we're exercising'
M comes over and joins them,
J: 'right,' he points at the other 2 children, 'you have 2 shots then it's me and B. again okay?

Figure 4.9 Observation (12th May) demonstrates the usefulness of the punch ball

We opened the doors and had outdoor milk and structured play – the children were all very good. Took some of our maths outside. There was only one slight hiccup when E momentarily wandered out of sight but the outdoor group took his hand and showed him the boundaries.

Figure 4.10 Personal journal extract 6th September

Extension into Primary 1 (Age 5–6)

Developed through further reflection in primary 1, the parachute activities became a particular favourite for class celebrations such as golden time (see Figure 4.6).

The children were eager to try circle time inside the parachute dome (see Photo 4.15), however they quickly expressed feelings of heat and claustrophobia. Anxious to follow up their idea, B suggested propping the parachute up on benches, this led to an extended lesson in group problem solving, the solution was then shared with the other infant class who loved the idea and were keen to 'have a go'.

Some time later returning to reflect on my journal entry (Figure 4.7) it occurred to me to try the circle time dome outside where it might be more airy, an activity which was indeed successful and very popular when we tried it out. Some of our favourite parachute activities are explained on Resource Sheet 4.4.

Photo 4.18 The bushes adorned with streamers

Outdoor Play

Nursery Intervention (Age 3–5)

The outdoors is a significant and often under-used learning environment according to Bilton (2002). In our nursery, outdoor play holds an important part in each day and is carefully planned to develop skills in all areas of the curriculum.

The observation in Figure 4.8 demonstrates the children's developing skills in communication and observation. Considering Emotional Literacy here was then a natural progression. One morning the children asked to play with a soft 1m inflatable ball, on an impulse this was hung from a tree forming a punch bag. This spontaneous activity facilitated endless opportunity for negotiation, emotional expression and discussion between the children. Previously I would not have encouraged any form of aggressive play but I had come to realise that this might support pupil development of emotional understanding and resilience (see Figure 4.9).

P1 Extension (Age 5–8)

Outdoor play changes dramatically in the primary 1 situation, and required considerable reflection on previous action to find a way forward. We are fortunate to have direct outdoor access from our class and this has allowed class activities to take place outdoors on dry days. It has also required the development of cooperative, trusting relationships where pupils take responsibility (Rogers, 1969), important in the development of Emotional Literacy (see Figure 4.10).

Developing my approach I have regularly spent time playing outdoors with the children to model play, inclusion and to reinforce its important role within the school day, for example:

- Activities to raise awareness of personal space and tolerance of accidental bumps: bubble blowing, collecting and playing with leaves, streamers to blow in the wind.
- Games to develop group rule agreement: shadow tig, follow my leader, ball and hoop games, what's the time Mr Wolf?
- Cooperative team building activities: using the parachute outdoors, communal skipping, snowman building, and obstacle courses.

Further simple activity ideas are provided in Resource 4.5, Ideas for 'A Pocket of Instant Fun'.

The playground observation in photograph 4.18 shows the bushes outside our classroom adorned with streamers at the end of play. Is this a form of ownership?

In this chapter, I have described activities which could be extended to develop Emotional Literacy. Chapter 5 now goes further to discuss the implications for the teacher in successfully developing Emotional Literacy and the need for the support of parents and the whole school community.

Further Reading

I found *Outdoor Play in the Early Years: Management and Innovation* by Helen Bilton a useful book. Also helpful is *Inspiring Inclusive Play,* which is the result of an action research project carried out by Casey et al. in 2004.

If you are new to circle time then *Quality Circle Time* by Jenny Mosley would be a good place to start.

For older children *Circle Time Sessions for Relaxation and Imagination* by Tony Pryce (2007) introduces meditation or *Into the Garden of Dreams: Pathways to Imagination for 5–8s* by L. J. Simpson (2001), also deals with relaxing, self esteem and expression.

The SEAL emotions cards are available at: www.edu.dudley.gov.uk/primary/SEAL/SEALbox/photocards/photocards.pdf

Electronic Resources

Go to www.sagepub.co.uk/christinebruce for electronic resources for this chapter:

4.1 Circle Time Lesson

4.2 Small World Play

4.3 Wanted Poster and Resource Sheets

4.4 Parachute Games

4.5 Ideas for 'A Pocket of Instant Fun'

4.6 Ideas to Establish Creative Outdoor Fun

4.7 Games Instructions

The Role of the Adult

In this chapter, I consider:

- **The opportunity provided by the project to develop and support in-class communication, and also crucially to develop a partnership with families in building and improving communication**
- **Suggestions for ways to involve parents more in the process, and develop their understanding of Emotional Literacy ('Parents' also mean guardians and carers)**
- **The benefits of taking a whole-school approach through raising awareness in Emotional Literacy.**

General Points

In teaching and supporting Emotional Literacy we need to first consider our own understandings of both what it is and its relevance in this context. Earlier chapters in this book go some way to addressing this. From the outset I stated that I believe Emotional Literacy is an approach which we develop. It is unique to each of us depending on our life experience and is a skill which we work towards along a lifelong continuum of learning experiences. It sits upon self reflection and through social interaction reaches forward to empathise with others. As adults we have a responsibility to our children who emulate our words and actions, and so we need to consider the implications of what we say and do.

Changes to our learning environment and teaching approach have been discussed. However, there are other little changes to the way we think and respond which, with practice, can also have a huge impact. The manner in which we phrase comments and responses supports positive, encouraging environments. For example, we can use positive requests such as 'Could you put that paper in the eco bucket please?' Instead of 'Don't drop that paper'. When a child falls most adults will say something along the lines of 'up you jump, give it a rub' and 'there it's all better now ...'. Have you fallen recently? A wee rub may help but does not take the pain away and heal the knee! A more emotionally literate response would empathise with the child while acknowledging the continuing discomfort and possible indignity which they are feeling.

To Think About:

- *Why involve parents?*

The Role of Parents

It is natural that every parent wants the best for their child and as children spend a lot of time in school, teachers, also naturally, expect parents to be interested in what happens there. Moreover, encouraging the interest and input of parents is crucial and is often considered singularly significant in improving educational achievement. Their influence carries on to impact on life success (Harris & Goodall, 2008). We know, for example, that from an early age behaviour is influenced by role models and parenting styles (Brown & Dunn, 1996) and that inadequate parenting leads to anti-social school behaviour. This in turn is linked to poor academic progress and peer rejection. Serbin et al. (1991) suggest further that aggressive/anti-social children grow in to inadequate parents thus creating a negative cycle.

Emotions themselves can also become a barrier to home–school partnership through parents' past negative experiences with education. Often the only way to overcome this is through first addressing the parent's own learning needs. It is worth taking the time in overcoming these in order to work together and think how their children can grow emotionally and academically. There are other barriers which we need to overcome, such as English as a second language, or a teacher's over-reliance on educational jargon. The key to successful inclusive practice would be a barrier-free community, which, as Frederickson & Cline (2009) discuss, promotes collaboration and equality in partnership with parents.

Overcoming Barriers

Below I have listed some suggestions which we or other schools have found helpful.

- A soft start to the school day where parents are invited to arrive within a specified time block and come in to chat and play. Thirty minutes works well in the pre-school setting, where 10–15 minutes can be adequate in a school setting. This also provides an ideal time for parents to discuss and add to their child's scrapbook, which documents their progress both in and out of school.

- A welcoming meeting space for parents where staff also join in and talk about nursery/school plans. I heard of one nursery who kept their washing machine in this area and parents would stay and help or chat while doing their laundry.

- Home visits to families, school or pre-school, who don't attend parents' open evenings.
- Parents' workshops with an emphasis on a friendly and relaxed atmosphere. These can often be targeted to specific groups.
- A home school support worker.
- Fathers only meetings.
- Family open evenings with specific ethnic/cultural themes.
- Transition meetings held as a family/school outing with nursery and primary 1 parents, children and staff. A relaxed opportunity for everyone to get to know each other.
- Regular chatty newsletters which incorporate reports and requests written or illustrated by the children.
- Daily news bulletins posted at the entrance which let people know what is happening each day and which support parent–child discussion.
- Letters home requesting background information including parental interests (see Resource 2.2).
- Personalised invitations to open evenings, meetings, etc., through asking the children to make and or illustrate invitations.
- Organised coffee meetings with talks from local partners in education. I have found all of the following partners very helpful and eager to come in to work with parents or their toddlers. The meetings bring parents together and from there they can establish ownership to develop interests further, either individually or in groups.
  - The community nurse or health visitor – sessions on concerns raised by parents, for example on children's eating fads, sleep patterns, or baby massage.
  - Someone from the local sports centre – to run a 'taster' session.
  - The active schools coordinator – what's available locally and what you can do as a parent to keep your children healthy and active.
  - The park ranger – activities for parents to encourage and interest young children.
  - Heart start – emergency fist aid.
  - The librarian – story telling for toddlers or parents workshop.
  - Other parents – to talk about their work or interests.

What is Partnership?

In defining school culture Durrant & Holden (2006) highlight the importance of the quality of relationships both within the school itself, and with its families and the wider community beyond. They see a school culture as a complex set of attitudes, beliefs and values which can determine the overall quality of learning taking place. However, it can be argued (Walker & MacLure, 2005; Austin, 2007; Todd, 2007) that the partnership presently offered to parents and school friends is little more than a 'token gesture' within the existing school system. Building successful partnerships requires concerted effort, time and commitment from both parents and schools. Harris & Goodall (2008) warn that it will not happen unless parents know the difference they make and know that they really matter. Their support needs to be a central priority and integral to school planning. At present there is little effort by schools to plan real contexts where parents can offer genuine and appropriate learning experiences, and little, if any, regard for how parents or friends can achieve something in return. How much better it could be to look at and build-in centrally the wealth of experience from the homes of our pupils at the planning stage. Austin suggests that the separation of the rich and individual contextual learning which takes place in homes from the standardised curricular learning in school can set children at a disadvantage which they must bridge themselves. This bridging can require a huge effort for some children, providing yet another barrier to learning.

Partnership is built on mutual respect and understanding. If the school finds a child has a particular learning need then the parents or carers must be consulted. The resulting partnership provides an opportunity to share supportive strategies in both directions. A family may provide invaluable advice and physical support. Together collaborative plans can be made with all services: education, health, social work, visiting specialist teachers, educational psychologist, support assistant and support for learning teacher. From a parent's perspective any multi-professional meeting could be a daunting, perhaps overwhelming, experience, so it is worth suggesting that they should bring a friend for some moral support. Harris (2007: 5) suggests that inclusion requires us to *'transcend'* the Emotionally Literate model of Goleman (1996) and form more creative relationships which also *'acknowledge our vulnerabilities and cultivate and refine our strengths'*. In support of parental partnership Shah (2001) believes we should have high expectations of all members of the community and make clear that their support raises attainment. For some parents this partnership might take the form of supporting or leading extracurricular activities or sports clubs. The EYFS Principles into practice card 1.4 recognises this, stating that *'Children feel a sense of belonging in the setting when their parents are also involved in it'*. (DCSF, 2008)

Homework

Findings suggest that schools need to support and build home–school relationships with both those parents who are already involved as well as reaching out to the rest, *'most of all schools need to shift to encouraging parental engagement of learning in the home through providing levels of guidance and support'* (Harris & Goodall, 2008: 286). Often schools are guilty of failing to give adequate guidance to parents in how to support children in getting the best from a homework experience. In a social realignment, Walker & MacLure (2005) feel the Parents Charter now places an educational 'responsibility' on parents and *The Children's Plan* (DCSF, 2007: 6) states further that *'Families are the bedrock of society and the place for nurturing happy, capable and resilient children'.*

To Think About:

- *Are you providing true partnership with families in learning and teaching?*
- *Are you providing homework which is a worthwhile experience?*

Homework can support communication with the home through creative and personalised activities which families can work on together. However, just as what goes on at home can affect a child's in-school learning, we sometimes forget that the converse, what goes on in school, can have a significant implication for a family. Homework is only one such issue where some parents, working long hours, quite understandably may resent the intrusion into their precious time together as a family; particularly if homework is mundane, repetitive or perhaps on the face of it, even pointless. Parents may have significant anxieties about approaching the teacher to discuss this and while under considerable emotional pressure to be a 'good parent' become resentful. Resulting tensions between home and school environments are not uncommon, with the child caught in the middle, the often tenuous learning opportunity is then lost. In fact an argument is raised by McCarthy (2005) that homework deepens inequalities and the class divide while there is little or no evidence that supports the benefits. When creating an Emotionally Literate school policy for partnership it is important to include homework flexibility and properly acknowledge alternative points of view.

Pupil achievements both within and out of the school also need celebration and acknowledgement. Just as best school work and achievements deserve recognition, equally it is important to provide space within class to display set homework which gives this proper in-school recognition and celebrates home partnership work.

The school website can be a great support to communication of homework tasks, with each class having its own page for explaining homework. If set homework is considered boring, consider setting home learning challenges which are personal to the child's needs and interests. However, it is important to bear in mind the inequality of resources available across homes such as internet access, books, parental education or attitude, and simple resources such as pencils, desks or a quiet space. These inequalities create unfair divisions in home learning and support. It is possible also that it is grandparents or other carers in charge at homework time. Glasgow & Hicks (2003: 2) remind us that *'homework is one of our most entrenched institutional practices, yet one of the least investigated'.*

Parent Meetings

Both classroom environments and teaching approaches will have undoubtedly changed since most parents were at school. This in itself presents enormous barriers to communication and understanding which, if ignored or unresolved, inevitably heighten anxiety and frustration amongst parents. However, there is a great deal that parents know and can do, particularly with regard to their own children. This makes them an important and potentially invaluable resource, which Atkin et al. (1988) believe most schools fail to utilise effectively. Many parents simply lack the confidence to make the most of their knowledge, missing a unique opportunity.

It is crucial then that we take time to listen to and explore what parents have to share with us in developing what Atkin et al. (1988: 18) describe as *'a mutually relaxed and beneficial working partnership'* since this is the key to planning teaching which matches specific needs and will *'engage meaningful parental participation and involvement'*. As professionals we can then suggest practical developments while learning new and alternative ways of working.

There is no such thing as a perfect parent nor a perfect teacher and as Shah (2001) describes, each may approach a meeting feeling defensive, accountable or even inadequate, both however want what they believe is best for the child and they will need to share that responsibility. A parent invests a great deal emotionally in their child and may feel their input is undervalued. They may have avoided approaching the teacher until a given situation has built out of proportion. Through keeping communication frequent and open an emotionally charged and volatile situation may be avoided.

Have you considered how the classroom looks and feels from the parents' viewpoint? Walker & MacLure (2005) describe parents' meetings like visiting a doctors' surgery! Obvious considerations such as your welcome, seating arrangements, and what you are wearing all set the tone for the meeting and can make less of a 'clinical' barrier. During the project I experimented with the ambience for our meetings. Having considered an informal seating arrangement I'd ask you to also consider lighting, scent and sound. Our parents appreciated subdued lighting, our classroom scent and some background music.

To Think About:

- *How do you welcome parents?*
- *Is your style of communication with parents a barrier?*

The Role of Support Staff

The role of all staff is of immense importance in creating and maintaining an Emotionally Literate school and none more so than the support staff who often work more closely with individual children who experience significant barriers in class or less structured school times. Mutual respect conveyed through their attitude, body language and handling of situations can make the difference in achieving a caring and respectful environment where children can develop resilience and independence in safety and security. The training of support staff of all types is therefore essential; you simply will not achieve your desired goal if the whole school community is not on the same wavelength. A useful resource here may be the recent work of Margaret Collins (2009) *Raising Self-Esteem in Primary Schools.*

In-class support needs careful reflection, planning and evaluation to take the best advantage of time and individual talents. Time should be planned in for exchange of strategies, skills and progress information. Where time for talk is constrained, an in-class running notebook to exchange information must be kept between teacher and support which explains objectives, teaching strategies and provides space for evaluative feedback.

Often support staff have to deal with issues which occur when the class are outdoors, and for them to undertake their role effectively they need the support of not only the teaching staff but also the parents. There is simply no point in putting a class outside to play and then disappearing to the staff coffee room, without some exchange of information which might support a 'happier' and more peaceful playtime.

Involving Parents and Families

If parents or grandparents, like support staff, are to be successfully utilised then they need the mutual respect of all members of the school community. Remember that children copy the role models they see around them, they will watch to see how each of us interact and communicate with each other. Hammond (2007) believes parents and practitioners should work together to plan not only in-class learning but also natural and rich learning in the outdoors where children will fully engage in their learning.

Break time is part of the school day and, as such, a learning opportunity which should be planned and prepared for. By this I do not suggest withdrawing the children's 'free' and spontaneous time, however, I believe social skills, playground games and rhymes and friendship, resolution and anti-bullying skills all need to be taught as part of the Emotionally Literate and PSE programme. I find playtime or break can be a period of anxiety for many children and for just as many parents. There are a number of things we can do to support this.

Parents and grandparents can support break through:

- working on school ground improvements with groups of children during the school day, at break times or after school
- running activities such as a gardening club in the school grounds
- attending training workshops to learn and share playground games and skills which teach and encourage resilience

- joining break time play as play leaders. This can be as much fun for parents as for the children
- fundraising to resource and maintain playground equipment such as boxes containing skipping ropes, balls, hoops and marbles as well as larger more expensive general playground items
- organising wide games like treasure hunts (I have a bag of stones painted like ladybirds for hiding which have been enormously popular. I also have sets of laminated teddy bears and pirate galleons for similar games)
- sitting in a quiet area and hosting activities such as story telling or environmental art
- running playground challenges. See also Resource 4.5 'A Pocket of Instant Fun'.

Playtime is an area where parental input is invaluable, particularly in the first school year when there is a huge difference in the available resources between the nursery outdoor play area and the school play area. Older children can be a great help here in alleviating parental worries. In preparation for the transition, older children acting as 'buddies' can take nursery children to the big playground during playtime to support them in getting used to the idea and how to use the space.

Times of transition provide an ideal opportunity to work with parents (Shah, 2001) since they have a particularly high level of interest at this point. Most schools organise an assortment of transition activities including class visits and school tours with older pupils as guides. There is usually an induction meeting where lots of information is distributed but it is also worth considering making individual meetings and home visits available. As teachers we are used to the school environment, however, for some parents this can be a traumatic time in strange surroundings and with unfamiliar people. It is worth taking a moment to reflect on the reception they receive: is the entrance friendly and inviting? Being relaxed and demonstrating natural empathy, active listening and providing space to talk and ask questions is all important.

Fathers are a particularly under-utilised resource and, as Garner & Clough (2008) point out, many fathers want to be more involved in their children's education but are restricted by work commitments and a lack of confidence. Research has proven that their relationships in particular can impact on achievement, however they need specific encouragement and welcome into our schools and nurseries. Some suggestions given by Garner & Clough include father-friendly newsletters and activities which specifically use male directed language, training workshops for fathers, and fathers-only events such as a Fathers in School day. It is worth making an explicit policy statement valuing the involvement of fathers.

The Role of the Teacher

Teachers use their emotions continuously throughout their day, they are central to our work which can leave us feeling 'drained' at the day's end. This use of emotion can be helpful or harmful, either in raising or in lowering classroom standards, building relationships with colleagues and partnerships with families. Emotions are part of being a human and the capacity for teachers to use their emotions well in the workplace according to Hargreaves (2000), comes down to the quality of our emotional understanding. In this sense, more widespread Emotional Literacy may depend not only on quality relationships but also on distributing power and responsibility more widely through giving/taking the opportunity for greater 'voice'.

To Think About:

- *What are the qualities of an Emotionally Literate teacher?*

Here are some ideas of what an Emotionally Literate teacher might be and I'm sure you could add more of your own.

An Emotionally Literate teacher:

- is reflective and uses these reflections to inform their learning journey
- plans with the pupils' interests at the centre
- considers the uniqueness of every human
- inspires, and models, what they preach
- is someone whom we wish to emulate
- has high yet realistic social and academic expectations
- will demonstrate the ability to listen with sincerity, concern and care
- will empower those around them
- appreciates knowledge comes from many sources – pupils, parents, colleagues, and the community, as well as from books or the internet
- will create, maintain and emanate a positive aura.

This is a pretty tall order, however, an Emotionally Literate teacher above all knows that good teaching is more of a journey than a destination. I have the Optimist's Creed (see Further Reading) firmly placed at the side of my desk! I also keep a personal empowering statement beside my bed. As Harris (2007) states, we have a duty of care to our own emotional wellbeing.

The importance of self belief and a positive self image underlies excellence and cannot be stressed enough. Teachers praising, supporting and encouraging each other has been proved to encourage better teaching and improve pupil self esteem.

Every teacher needs to ensure they leave time and space within their busy lives for maintaining their personal wellbeing. This is something we can all participate in supporting and strengthening in each other, for an Emotionally Literate teacher will build strong and positive relationships with their colleagues. It's easy to tell children what to do, but we need to model it personally for it to be effective! A positive forward-looking person will not see a bunch of problems on the horizon but rather a host of opportunities.

To nurture our own Emotional Literacy and support colleagues involves reflection and the resulting *'recognition of who you are and choosing what you do'* (Sharp, 2001: 29). As teachers build an emotionally literate community, trust and understanding develops between colleagues which will encourage critical debate. There is a message here for parents too, if they want their child to be emotionally stable then they too need space to reflect. The values which underpin your pedagogy, what and how you think about children and education are fundamental to the kind of teacher you are and the learning experiences you provide for your children. As Crozier & Reay (2005) and Cox (2005) support, your demeanour towards your pupils and expectations of them, will have a powerful influence upon their motivation and progress.

Teachers also have a responsibility to be aware of the wide-ranging barriers to children's learning. In responding to children's needs, we must be able to work collaboratively, exchanging ideas and strategies in multi-agency meetings with a range of professionals who represent not only education but also health and social work. New skills and greater understanding will be required by all involved in this process.

As influential role models we have a further responsibility to admit with good grace when we are wrong so that children can learn to do this too. Being able to admit to and learn from our mistakes is an important part of resilience. We need to be able to listen to children and encourage them to talk about their concerns without being judged.

The Importance of Teacher Self Esteem

Teachers are powerful role models in children's lives and should take care to value each child just as they are. Gottman (1997) writes that children come to school with the belief that they can learn, surely it is then up to us to support and nourish that self belief, not squash it. In writing 'The Emotional Experience of Teaching' Hanko (2002) concludes that the more teachers interact with pupils, the more they come to understand and accept them, and the greater the individual learning potential. Teachers who really listen to children and look beyond the surface, avoid emotional misunderstandings, and can, as Hargreaves (2000) suggests, then work to improve the self esteem, behaviour and learning motivation of the individual child. We can raise pupil self esteem through employing firm, fair boundaries and by providing opportunities for differing learning styles and participative decision-making, as discussed in Chapter 2 (page 23). More than this I would stress the power of maintaining a relaxed and happy environment built on sound partnerships. If independence and peer support are encouraged then each child becomes confident of their own unique contribution to the class. Children will thrive when each small personal achievement is acknowledged and they feel a valued member of the class community.

The effect of teacher self esteem should not be underestimated. As previously discussed in Chapter 3 (see page 43), self esteem should be considered a core element in the development of Emotional Literacy. If troubled children use much of their emotional energy to cope with their problems, then so equally do troubled teachers. Roberts (1995) asserts that teachers, through developing their own sense of self can raise pupil self esteem. Teachers supporting their peers has been proved not only to improve teaching but to also improve pupil self esteem (Fullan, 1991; Lawrence, 1996). I believe that if we want to raise attainment then each of us needs to feel a valued part of the school community.

Attachment

Cooper (2008) explains that inclusion is based on social and emotional attachment which can only be achieved when the whole school put emotional wellbeing at the heart of all that they do. Teacher–pupil relationships are complex and we know they play a key role, not simply in learning but in the whole school experience. Studies exploring the role of the teacher in Emotional Literacy are limited yet, as Perry et al. (2008) support, teachers are widely accepted as *'significant others'*. This is important when figures from the NSPCC state that although 9 out of 10 children have a warm and loving family background, 1 in 10 children suffer from serious abuse or neglect at home and the British Medical Association (2006) estimates that 20% of children experience mental health problems.

Geddes (2006) explains further that children with strong, healthy attachments are more resilient, able to settle, and eager to explore and find out about the world. Conversely, children who are less secure and dominated by attachment anxieties can exhibit a range of problems. Often in such cases the needs of the mother have taken priority over the needs of the child. Morton (2004) suggests using story as a therapy in supporting attachment behaviour problems. In this way the teacher can act as a bridge to the outside world through providing one reliable, supportive and consistent approach.

Working as a Collaborative Team

Harris (2007: 6) writes that *'The emotional work of leadership involves facilitating and supporting each person's active engagement in meaningful dialogue, deep learning and collaborative agency'* – only then will the educational community thrive. The voice of the school should be inclusive and collective in every respect. Much can be achieved simply through the language and attitudes within the 'hidden curriculum'. It is vital to say, for example, our school, our class, our children and our friends, as it is that within the team the voice of the child is heard, recognised and heeded.

Children, and particularly children with disabilities, have until now had little say in plans made on their behalf. If we truly aspire to real inclusion then it is important that their voice is not only heard but listened to. In an Emotionally Literate school the voice from the bottom is heard. The 'bottom-up' approach described in Fullan (1993) must work in partnership with the 'top-down' approach to marry the best ideas and strategies to achieve successful, quality inclusion. However, Fullan (1993: 26) points out that the *'legal and financial structures must be in place to support the initiatives and enable them to succeed'*. As Todd (2007) discusses, collaborative working between children, young people, families and professionals is key to the government's long-term strategy to promote the wellbeing of children, including more inclusive education.

The Whole-School Approach

The EL approach is sensitive to the needs of individual children, and develops a sense of belonging, self esteem and social skills through a whole-school approach. As Cooper (2008) argues, schools which succeed have a strong community which values and celebrates success for each pupil in all their diversity, not simply the top academic achievers. This approach includes all supporting and ancillary staff in developing pupil responsibility and resilience. It is vital to acknowledge that rejection often leads to further aggression, and to work on the premise that bad behaviour is usually intended to meet a legitimate need; it is the pupils' choice of self management strategy which can be problematic. Through group work children can build a bank of alternative responses and thereby resilience and responsibility can be improved. It has been said that if there was less anger experienced by both pupils and staff there would be less problem behaviour. Emotional Literacy can develop a greater sense of perspective through learning empathy and tolerance of difference in others. It increases our ability to relate to different types of people. Creating a sense of belonging is the most effective way to establish and maintain community for everyone.

To Think About:

- *What do we mean by the term 'whole-school'?*
- *What would an Emotionally Literate school be like?*

This is a good question to ask your colleagues at school. Our school staff thought it was a school where: all the members of the school community felt valued and respected; there was clear and open communication within a supportive and caring environment; and where staff and pupils encourage each other and greet each other with a friendly smile.

It is also a community where

- teachers have high expectations of their children
- fairness and justice are seen to be upheld
- opportunities to succeed are planned and celebrated
- everyone has clear roles and responsibilities
- positive behaviour strategies are a shared responsibility
- parents and friends are warmly welcomed

Photos 5.1 a and b An Emotional Literacy display of pupil work takes a central place at the school entrance. The area includes a book for pupils to record their thoughts and feelings along with a post box for more personal thoughts or problems which they wish to discuss in private

- collegiate consultation and dialogue are the norm
- pupil forums are taken seriously and pupil voice genuinely respected
- strong positive discipline is based on mutual respect
- there is pride in the school community
- a clear anti-bullying message encourages independence and resilience
- there is a sense of fun and creativity.

It is a recipe where no single element makes the whole, but just as in life, each individual must work together as part of that whole to succeed. Weare (2004: 105) describes it as a *'dynamic equilibrium between several different elements'*. Just as in an individual class environment small changes put together can have a huge impact, so can the whole school in creating a team.

One suggestion for whole-school team work is the circle time approach to Emotional Literacy timetabled across the school for a Monday morning, as discussed in Chapter 4 (see page 46). The management team can then keep time free to follow up any sensitive issues which need time and space outwith the classroom.

In discussing the whole-school team this of course should include the pupils, who must become active partners in planning their learning, actively involved in the move towards a community, based on open dialogue and genuine collaboration. Fullan (2003) argues forcibly that just as successful commercial enterprises now place a high premium on knowledge creation and transfer, so we in education must do the same. It is through social interaction that mere information is transferred into knowledge and it is through sustained interaction, he argues, that knowledge

Photo 5.2 Every nook or cranny can be used to raise EL awareness

becomes wisdom and 'deep change' becomes a possibility. Interaction itself is not sufficient; Fullan highlights the danger of so-called communities of learning simply reinforcing underperformance and argues that the way to avoid this is to unlock and engage the passion and commitment of all members of a community.

To Think About:

- *How EL am I?*
- *How do I find out?*

Further Reading

Parents as Partners in their Children's Learning: Toolkit

www.scotland.gov.uk/Resource/Doc/147410/0038822.pdf

The Children's Plan: Building Brighter Futures

www.dcsf.gov.uk/childrensplan/downloads/The_Childrens_Plan.pdf

The Optimist Creed

www.optimist.org/e/visitor/creed.cfm

Implications for Practice

In this chapter, I consider:

- **The project research findings**
- **The implications for practice**
- **The benefits and pitfalls of doing research in practice.**

Throughout this book I hope you will have noticed that a lot of 'our' and 'we' statements have been made. This is because in an Emotionally Literate school climate we all look out for each other. It is a way of establishing and maintaining belonging. So it is not my class – the class belongs to all of 'us'. The school is not 'my school' or 'theirs' but ours – all the children and staff and parents together who make the school community.

In 2004 we wrote that Emotional Literacy is:

> *a developed awareness and understanding of one's own and others emotions. This information guides our thinking and is expressed in our communication and behaviour. Further, it is the understanding that individuals feel emotions in different ways and therefore have different responses depending on their life experience.* (Parkhead Nursery Staff, 2004)

... but the way I see it now Emotional Literacy is more, it is:

> *a holistic recognition, understanding and consideration of the unique emotional interdependence of self and other. Emotional Literacy is an approach to life.*

During the period of the project I grew as a person and I hope improved as a teacher. Only the children, however, can answer that in the years to come, because it will only be with time that the results will, or perhaps will not, show. The most important thing I learned was that I have still got much more to learn. The EL approach doesn't happen overnight – no change does.

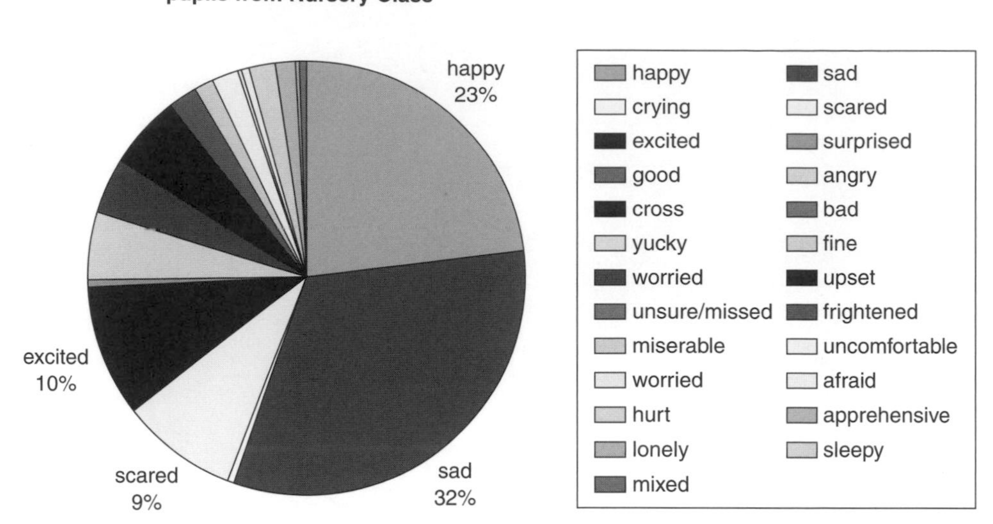

Figure 6.1 Results of the P 1a pupil interview, October

Collected Data

The data discussed here was gathered over a nine-month period through reapplying the initial research instruments as outlined in Chapter 1 (page 10). The purpose was to assess the impact of the programme on children's social behaviour and in meeting the original objectives outlined in Resource 1. Every attempt to 'build out' invalidity was taken at each successive stage in order to give confidence and credence to the research. Construct validity was carefully considered in the initial preparatory stages including jury validity in the construction of a collaborative definition for Emotional Literacy.

Pupil Interviews

The pupil vocabulary interviews were undertaken in the October with 'puppet' support and focused on the emotional vocabulary of the 19 nursery children who continued into their first school year in primary 1a. Although this was a small sample group the data were quite clearly and significantly more varied – see Figure 6.1 – with 55% of the children now only using either happy or sad compared to 90% just nine months previously, undoubtedly demonstrating a greater emotional vocabulary base in the group.

The results raised some questions:

- How much of this increase was simply due to maturity?
- Would the children have reached this point around this time anyway without the intervention?
- Was the increase due as much to changed parental use of language with their children as to the intervention?

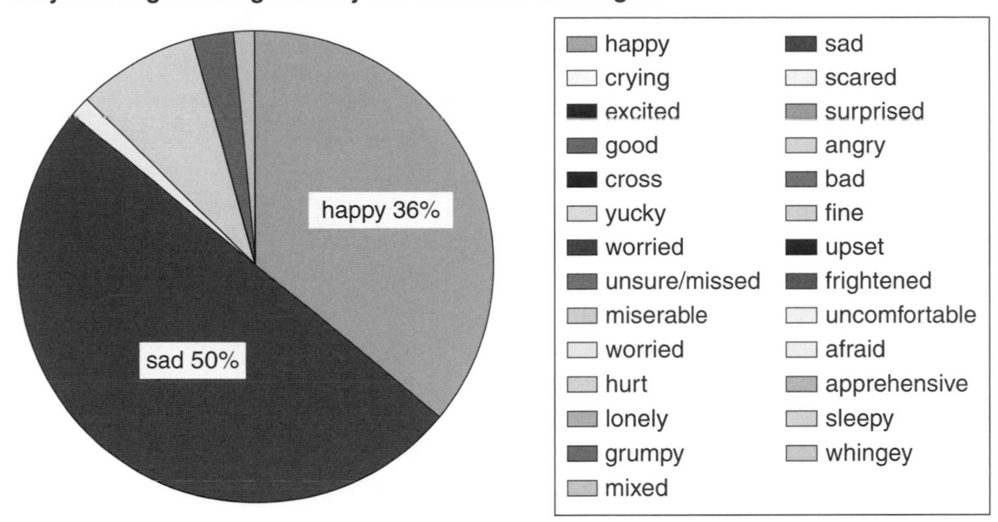

Figure 6.2 Neighbouring nusery data, May

The six pupils who joined the new 1a class from a neighbouring nursery provided an additional opportunity for comparison. Despite the weak sample size, the data supported the suggested notion that the intervention was making a positive difference. Figure 6.2 demonstrates that they gave an 86% response of happy/sad in the interview before entering school, similar to our nursery group at 90%, then the data gathered three months later, shown in Figure 6.3, shows a drop to 71%, which may be said to have been due to the three months of Emotional Literacy intervention activities in primary 1.

The Parent Questionnaire

The evaluation of the parent questionnaire returns highlight the breadth of vocabulary used by parents compared to their children – see Figure 6.4. This may have been due to a design failing in the questionnaire, with parents misinterpreting the intention as either to discover:

- words the child would actually use, or
- words the parents used to describe children's emotions.

There was also a drop in the variety of words parents used over the nine-month period. However, in expressing the data as a percentage there was also a drop in happy/sad responses from 36% to 25%. Is this an indication that the project was reaching beyond the school gates? Seventy-six schedules were distributed to the same initial parents at the end of the project with 32 of these returned. Nine months earlier 35 schedules were returned which suggests the level of parental interest in the project was maintained across both data collections and could be interpreted as an indication that the parents enjoyed being included, as indeed the note from a parent at the beginning of the project, shown in Figure 6.5 demonstrates.

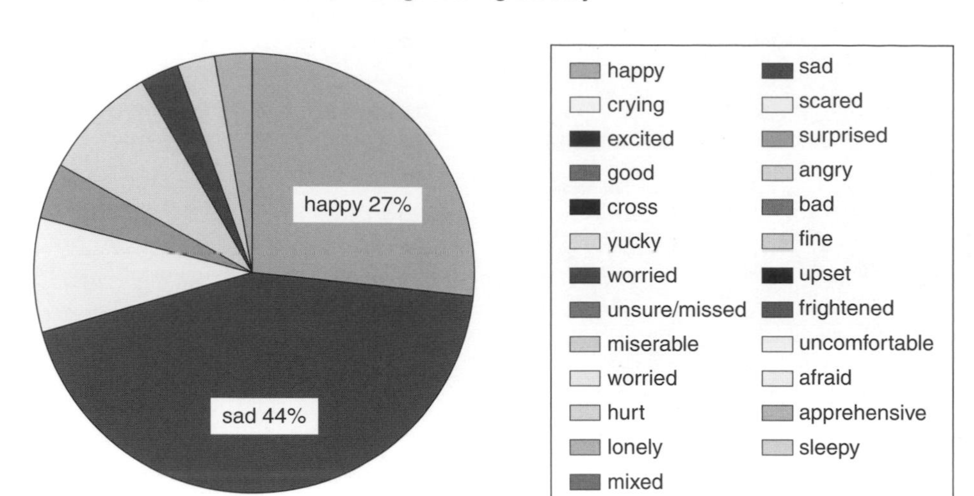

Figure 6.3 Neighbouring nursery data, October

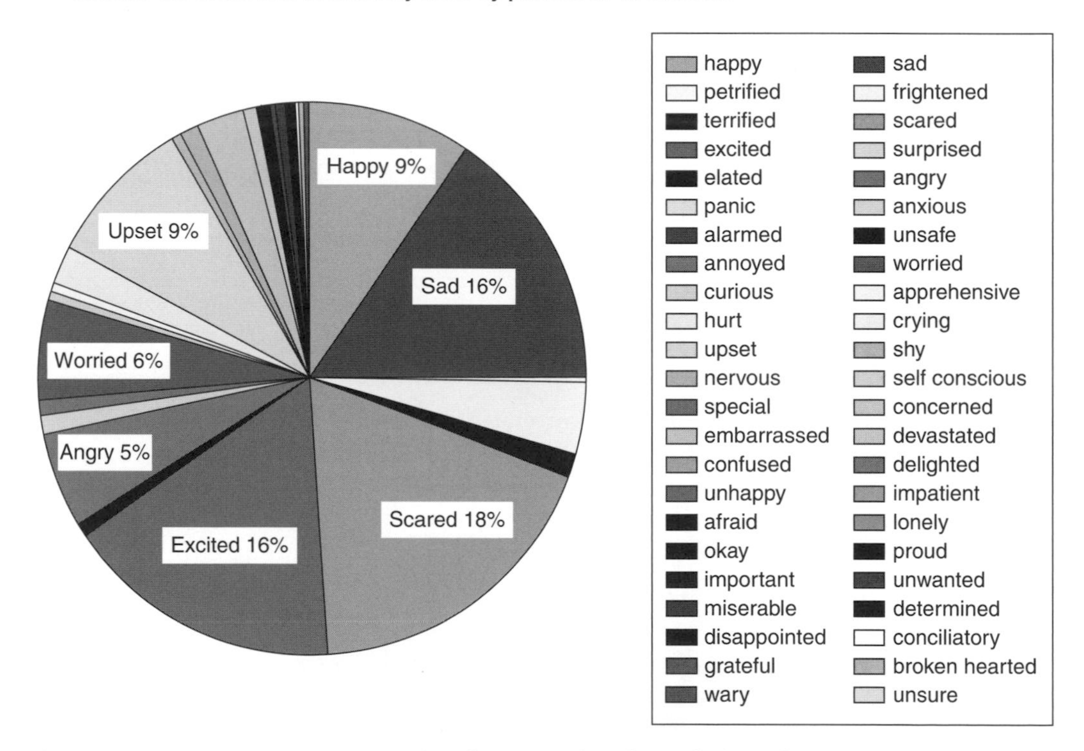

Figure 6.4 Parent questionnaire, October: emotional vocabulary data

This parental interest in itself must surely have been invaluable to the progress of the project as parents with a raised awareness would arguably have discussed more with their children. Figure 6.5 also further highlights the gap between the parents' perceived skills of their children, and the reality. As stated earlier, based on the adult response, it could be suggested that parents generally fail to appreciate the lack of

Thank you for taking the time to complete this information.

I enjoyed completing this with E. It was enlightening. She has a clear understanding of happy, sad and frightened. Yet scared, worried, excited, surprised were words she never used. She spoke about not being happy in a lot of situations where I might have expected her to say worried. In the case of all positive events she has experienced e.g. the night before going on holiday and meeting Cinderella at Euro Disney (a highlight for her) and everything was happy. It will be interesting to note any changes.

Figure 6.5 An example of parent interest through a comment added to an initial questionnaire

language skills which their children have and the difficulties this causes them in expressing their feelings and needs. Two school parent and child open evenings were planned during the project period which gave an opportunity to raise further awareness and general discussion while gathering informal feedback. During the second of these I was able to run a slide show showing the children working with emotional literacy activities and for the children to demonstrate the BBC interactive website www.bbc.co.uk/cbeebies/tikkabilla/games/emotion.shtml.

Facial Expression

In the same way, character drawings demonstrating facial expression were used with all the children both at the start of the nine-month period and again at the end to monitor the children's perception of expression. The resulting data from the 19 continuing children is shown here in Figure 6.6. The presented data may demonstrate limited progress, since there are clearly still many misunderstandings, however, in practice the greater ease with which the children sorted, categorised and named the expressions was obvious. In a similar situation Walden & Field (1982) found that overall older children made fewer mistakes but this did not materialise here. I can only presume that the children were now thinking more, rather than categorising everything as happy or sad. I conclude that children gradually learn that expressions are a complex combination of several facial features. I would like to think that we were supporting the growth of understanding in our children as we were going through this process – Figure 6.7 demonstrates this.

It could be argued that teaching and assessing emotional vocabulary does not demonstrate emotional understanding. This is quite possibly true, however it is also true that we are born wanting to communicate, our society depends on the use of language to communicate and it is important that we develop this to the fullest capacity. In support, Vygotsky (1978) argued that communication is central to child development. However, words alone can be misinterpreted, it is only through supporting body language and gesture that their full meaning is reached. Dunn et al. (2002) discuss the essential ability to use theory-of-mind correlated with communication skills during cooperative play or conflict resolution situations. Taking this one step further and developing the ability to empathise builds a crucial social skill, a skill which Cutting & Dunn (1999) and Scharfe (2000) assert can be developed pre-school.

Expression Cards Jan. 05: nursery 1a

Expression	Correct	Incorrect	Total
Happy	18	1	19
Sad	16	3	19
Excited	7	12	19
Angry	12	7	19
Surprised	4	15	19
Worried	2	17	19
Scared	9	10	19
Hurt/crying	11	8	19
Total	79	73	152

Expression Cards Oct. 05: primary 1a

Expression	Correct	Incorrect	Total
Happy	14	5	19
Sad	9	10	19
Excited	12	7	19
Angry	18	1	19
Surprised	10	9	19
Worried	14	5	19
Scared	18	1	19
Hurt/crying	12	7	19
Total	107	45	152

Figure 6.6 Expression recognition

PSD time – Anger was the subject they brought up for discussion again this morning. I let the children make angry expressions like in E's photo, then they made sentences to explain why they might be angry. We discussed how you know when somebody is angry and what an angry face looks like. Sm thought an angry face looked 'crumpled'! ☺ I couldn't have found a better word myself. I let four different children take photographs of four other children trying to make angry faces or expressions! Used the word 'expression', the children were delighted with it. We talked about listening time and how tiredness or a lack of space sometimes made people angry – I could/should have discussed similar emotions! – Next time perhaps? We played 'Squashed Bananas' as a follow up to talking about lack of space – a good opportunity to build resilience!! and then 'Line Up Choice' again – a definite favourite! Finished with singing One Elephant Came Out to Play – we all had great fun and a really good laugh. I felt in a really good mood, everyone settled to language tasks quickly and I got the reading sorted out.

[Games explained in Resource 4.7]

Figure 6.7 Personal journal extract re expressions

Observations

The observations were made during contexts of free social interaction and focused on the children's growing levels of confidence and independence to express feelings and opinions. Different methods of recording were employed by different members of staff but we all found trying to record speech against class background noise is difficult and time consuming. Reflecting on the writings of Walford (2001) who, unable to understand the Dutch language, found observing body language allowed him to see interaction between people more clearly, I tried this method. The results were very 'tangible' and positive as can be seen in the brief excerpt shown in Figure 6.8.

Colleagues around the school began to notice and comment that the primary 1 children were using positive behaviour strategies during social communication. They were observed to be demonstrating a raised emotional resilience and problem solving ability both in the playground and the lunch hall through using given strategies to sort problems out themselves. The difference was that the children had been given the time to discuss problems in an open and supportive class atmosphere which had encouraged and developed their skills in problem solving and resilience. The class activities developed their vocabulary and the skills to better

Pupil C –	*observed chatting, presumably negotiating, then patiently waiting his turn for a shot at the hammer game. A later chat confirmed this.*
Pupil M –	*noticing J was left out and encouraging him to participate.*

Figure 6.8 An observation using the approach of Walford (2001)

S had been making good progress in managing his temper but returning to school after an absence … was hit on the face by a ball just as the bell rang for the end of play and he had to line up. Crying with pain and distress his response was to turn and hit another child who was totally uninvolved. The difference was that when I spoke to S he could recognise, explain and understand the problem and knew what he had to do next. The other child was able to understand S's anger and accept his apology while not bearing a grudge.

Figure 6.9 All was not a bed of roses

Pupil A to Pupil C: '... C you know that's inappropriate behaviour for school, R won't like that. Please don't do it again darling.' – We might just be getting somewhere!!

Figure 6.10 A critical incident observed in the corridor

explain, recognise and understand social situations. All was not a bed of roses, however, as the incident in Figure 6.9 highlights, yet simultaneously proves that we were making progress.

Another critical incident observed between two pupils in a school corridor lightened my step – Figure 6.10. It demonstrates the profound effects teacher modelling can have towards developing an Emotionally Literate climate. I missed the initial incident between pupils R and C and observed simply this response by pupil A.

Surely with time the influence of this type of problem resolution will deepen and spread across the school community. We were handling situations with greater Emotional Literacy, thus achieving the objective of working towards an Emotionally Literate workplace. Despite the possible susceptibility of observer bias on these reflections they are also supported not only by the quantitative figures but, significantly, by the observations of my colleagues. In this way pupil Emotional Literacy was measured through vocabulary used and observed behaviour strategies.

Discussion of Research Effectiveness

The action plan was, as anticipated, refined with reflection and evolved according to the needs of the children, as the updated plan, Resource 1.4, shows, but nevertheless it has continued to consider the intended research question:

> *If emotional literacy becomes an explicit focus during the pre-school stage as part of daily small-group time and throughout the nursery activities, will this develop the children's ability to express their feelings, and to manage their own social behaviour?*

In working towards a more Emotionally Literate school it was my aim to embed Emotional Literacy into the nursery curriculum, to monitor progress and to reflect on practice, building a more caring and beneficial teaching and learning environment.

The action research approach proved highly appropriate, particularly due to the flexibility it allowed. The findings of my personal reflections arose through the action research cycle, which was used to reflect on and improve teacher practice and to support pupil programmes of work.

On several occasions during the research narrative, I have made reference to action taken on impulse. I would maintain that this is an integral part of early years teaching, and is based on practical experience. Indeed it is an important skill for any teacher to develop, where practitioners are required to reflect as they work. This notion of reflection in action is generally credited to Schon (1983). Where necessary, a teacher should be able to change direction, adapt planned activities or extend learning. It is often described as 'being able to think on your feet' and is a quality I await with anticipation when supporting student teachers. There is definitely a place for this alongside the deeper, almost therapeutic, process of later reflection on action.

The emphasis on the process of sharing practice with colleagues also attracted me to this model of action research. While sharing my experiences demonstrated consideration for others, I in fact received support and encouragement for my own practice, as well as important guidance and advice when I strayed. In my experience, without this collegiality teaching can easily become an isolated job. The process of sharing experiences builds a supportive and emotionally literate environment. Haddon et al. (2005) found that an Emotionally Literate environment was a reflection of the quality and value placed on the relationships within a school.

Interviews and Questionnaires

Although interviews and questionnaires were not the main research vehicles for this project they were important in developing a simple baseline and final comparison. The questionnaire and interview schedules were piloted, modified and had the advantage of being easily organised and administered. The responses, however, indicated that a more explicit letter would have supported a more concise and consistent response from the parent questionnaire. The presentation of the data as a pie chart has the advantage of conveying the information more effectively, allowing quick and easy interpretation. The data collected has limitations in demonstrating the level of Emotional Literacy, it could simply measure a greater pupil vocabulary and knowledge of social conventions without a deeper understanding. The positivity of the data however must be considered a step in the right direction.

Observations

Observation is an integral but very time consuming part of daily nursery practice, (Bruce, 2004; Nutbrown, 2006) and it was important that we were each clear about the purpose before starting. Inevitably we recorded some mundane scenarios and missed other useful incidents. Much data was discarded since one cannot always be in the right place at the right time. We also spent time adapting the recording format, aiming to achieve clear, informative observations. Finding sufficient time to sit together to discuss, reflect and evaluate our findings was crucial but difficult within staff working hours and at times required prioritisation over basic preparation. All of this process developed an important skill within the team in using the action research cycle.

Experimenting with alternative methods, I tried using audio tape but this was limiting in a busy and rather noisy environment and was quickly dropped as an observational tool in preference to video (Geldard & Geldard, 1997). I found recording useful but very time consuming, requiring later viewing, transcribing and editing. Certainly the observations videoed in the nursery garden were able to demonstrate a much more focused and positive account of interaction than had been my general impression. Video could also be shared with parents or used as evidence of the need for individual pupil support.

The best observational data, simply achieved yet providing detail, were gathered in primary 1 through the impressionistic style favoured by Walford (2001). The advantage here as a teacher researcher was that I could stand centrally, first taking a few moments to orientate on activities then let my attention settle on the movement and body language around a centre of play, picking up on the group mood. This less detailed view in terms of recorded vocabulary was much more relaxed and provided surprisingly rich and meaningful data, particularly when supported by a photograph. I have now found myself able to take just a few minutes to observe in this way on a more regular basis, recording a few notes in my journal for later reflection. This is a very practical and useful discovery since previously I have found it almost impossible to find time to observe in an infant classroom.

To Think About:

- *Do I take time to simply 'observe' my children?*
- *What method of observation works best for me?*
- *How do I use these observations?*

The Advantage of Reflection

Undertaking an action research project requires diligence to record constructive and objective reflections. My journal has become an indispensable aid to support personal reflection and organisation. Written reflection is a skill which takes time to undertake and time to develop and refine. For me this is an ongoing process. The most useful device I found here was to form questions as illustrated in the example journal entry in Figure 6.11. These questions ensured that reflection on action initiated change as discussed in Moon (1999), an extended example in Chapter 2 Figure 2.3 demonstrates the process over several days. This skill is a definite bonus to the class teacher when used alongside reflection in action, for which there is also an important place.

I have certainly found that writing these reflections can be very therapeutic, through slowing down and deepening the thinking process, and in this way developing

Dealing with a behaviour incident – G knocked down a patiently built tower.

**That worked well – but what did I do differently? Rather than asking him why did you do that? I asked .... How do you think X felt? He spent a long time building it. And... How do you feel now? I asked the group – What do you think G should do? – Do you think G feels sorry? Well let's help him .... and make it fun!*

Later I wrote:

**I'm taking a different perspective or angle!! It was more EL and it worked. I did make G stop and think. The other children were able to advise what to do and G did take responsibility. Group pressure at its best!!*

Figure 6.11 Asking questions to focus my journal reflections

systematic reflection and personal 'voice', as Moon (1999) suggests, while also supporting my personal wellbeing. This journal became a running commentary of day-to-day events in my teaching, recording observations and reflections, feelings and reminders, experiences and activities, evaluations and plans, conversations with staff and parents, anything which stood out in the day. It allowed an opportunity to put events into perspective, to clarify thoughts and focus attention. The process of reflecting and evaluating was the core of the action research and used to inform our next steps, to initiate change and improve teacher practice.

At various stages during the journey of the project I felt I was simply marking time, or worse entering into ever decreasing circles. There were times when as a teacher researcher in unfamiliar territory I felt out of my depth and overwhelmed by my ever increasing workload, the very situation Walford (2001) warns of. I was concerned that my reflections lacked depth. Was I getting to the root of the problem? Was EL an understanding of feelings, the ability to express feelings or an understanding of the language to express feelings? I took comfort and support in the comments of Bell & Opie (2002: 19) who wrote *'don't despair take a deep breath and keep on going'*. While discussing progress with a 'critical friend' (Campbell et al., 2004), it was suggested that instead of focusing on the progress of the children I might look at the progress of the adults. It was of course an obvious suggestion. In my hectic day do I model what I preach? Am I proactive in achieving my stated values? I try to be but the answer is no, not as much as I would like to be. Whitehead (1989) introduces this concept describing it as a *'living contradiction'*. This was deep reflection in learning about myself as both a teacher and as a person. Roberts (1995) describes the significance of our role in our pupils' lives, the positive impact exerted on building self esteem through demonstrating active listening, empathy, sensitivity and trust, of creating an environment where self esteem can be enhanced. This is a significance which also impacts, through modelling my values, on parents and colleagues. McGinley (2001) writes that a classroom can become *'an oasis of calm in a child's life'* – how true! Yet how much better it would be for the whole school community working together to create that special caring, inclusive environment. As Fullan (1991) asserts, change must come from and through the staff. Through reflection on practice I have learned to consider situations from the child's point of view and without guilt, but more with a sense of professionalism, decide to change direction in the knowledge that I'm doing the right thing.

Shiel, in Rogers (1969: 19) sums the situation up when describing in her diaries the realisation that the most valuable aspects of a child's growth were intangible,

Taken from journal entry 27th April – After a run-in with a colleague
– Little incidents can have a very big effect! I have a lot of work still to do on my inner confidence, being able to process and express/ vocalise feelings at the time – not fester for days over an incident like this. Do I ever domineer over children or other staff like this? – I hope not! Do I allow them time to respond? Do I listen?

Figure 6.12 It takes courage to reflect and listen sensitively to what one is experiencing

unobservable – *'yet one senses, a metamorphosis taking place'*. One ordinary nursery morning, a usually very quiet and introverted parent turned her face directly to mine and returned my greeting cheerily acknowledging me with her voice and her eyes! This was a small but critical moment (Tripp, 1993), notable on a personal level as a breakthrough. Somekh (1995: 347) states that the reflection process lies at the core of action research when it is used to deepen our understandings of the complex and rich interactions of social groups. Further, Rogers (1969) asserts that it takes courage to reflect and listen sensitively to what one is experiencing, the journal extract in Figure 6.12 demonstrates this point.

The reflective process presents a considerable opportunity for professional development, as Browne (2004) suggests, and Somekh (1995: 344), while rightly warning of the dangers of introspection, purports that the process enhances professionalism thereby improving teaching. With all of this I agree, but consistent and deep reflection is a tall order to meet. Constantly during the action research process I doubted the depth of my reflections and time was a persistent enemy. I could most certainly have done a better job had I not needed to consider all the other aspects and demands of my role; however without being 'in action' I would not have had the insider knowledge and reflective ability necessary to change my practice.

The Responsibilities of the Teacher (Communication)

In considering the purpose and audience of the project it has been important, as Somekh (1995) highlights, that it remains accessible to my colleagues and useful as a means of reflecting on personal classroom practice. To disseminate is after all an important element of action research in practice. Fullan (1991) purports that the degree of change from any intervention is strongly related to collegiality. Somekh (1995) stresses the importance of recognising teacher research not just for accreditation but also to contribute to public knowledge. Stenhouse (1975) believed that only when teachers were centrally involved in curriculum development would it be possible to develop the curriculum in any meaningful way. I certainly feel ownership for what has been happening in my classroom. In attempting to develop an Emotionally Literate school we have established a collective belief and understanding in the value of Emotional Literacy, holding this as the key influence in the successful interaction of both teaching and learning, as supported by Hanko (2002).

It was hoped that a possible by-product of the intervention, through teaching and modelling the skills to the children, would be to simultaneously raise the Emotional Literacy of the school community and to some extent this has certainly occurred. We hoped by keeping parents informed about the project progress, through newsletters, open evenings and everyday contact to raise their awareness and quietly encourage their involvement. It was also hoped that Emotional Literacy would spread through the school community and into the wider community beyond the school gates. In no way do I feel this project is complete, there is a long way to go and attitudes are not changed overnight, there are many hurdles to overcome. Colwell & Hammersley-Fletcher (2004) found that to sustain an Emotionally Literate climate where everyone felt valued this had to be worked on **daily**.

The Impact on Pupils and the School Community

Specifically, despite the difficulties in measuring Emotional Literacy, a few suggestive patterns emerged from the evaluations:

- A notable increase in pupil emotional vocabulary
- An observed increase in pupil self esteem
- An observed use of strategies for emotional resilience.

While qualitative in nature these statements are supported by the measured increase demonstrated in emotional vocabulary and the observations recorded from a variety of sources.

In general, pupils responded well to the focus and were ready to discuss and take on board the issues, with in many cases an unexpected maturity. However, the sample group numbers were small, the time-scale short and the extent of possible contributory factors too great to assert that there is any definitive trend. The effect of normal development in language and social communication skills learned within the existing nursery environment and the effect of the focus on parental use of language with their children, could both impact on the results. As already stated, change takes time and it could be several years before any significant fruition can be seen. In undertaking this project the activities have permeated the classroom environment so that I see everything in terms of emotional exchanges. I now firmly believe that to succeed, any Emotional Literacy programme must become an integral part of the curriculum. Weare & Gray (2002) among many others support this holistic approach.

Implications for Professional Practice

The positive findings of this project are due in no small part to changes in classroom practice:

- Through an approach to teaching and learning which became more sensitive to the difference in understanding and Emotional Literacy of individual children and individual members of staff.
- Through the organisation of groups which took account of social interaction and nurtured a sense of self esteem and belonging.

- Through a personal shift in attitude as a teacher both to time management and prioritisation of Emotional Literacy within the curriculum.
- Through the recognition that the perception of any situation by individual members of the team was different.

The question which should be asked here is would the same positive results be achieved by any other teacher? The response would suggest that while a specific resource, such as *Developing Baseline Communication Skills* by Delamain & Spring (2000), remained a useful and constant element as an underlying and supporting skeleton, the project was enhanced and brought alive by teacher enthusiasm. These interventions came about through a personal belief in the worth of Emotional Literacy and can only lead towards the conclusion that teacher attitude, enthusiasm and determination are to the largest extent behind the success of the programme, more so than the materials themselves. This is a finding which stems from the action research process of reflection on action and is supported by Medwell et al. (1998) and Fraser et al. (2001).

Overall, the research findings support the notion that the prioritisation of emotional understanding in relationships and in the teaching and learning process can have a positive impact on raising both individual self esteem and overall standards, as Hargreaves (2000: 824) endorses, and therefore should indeed be a core feature of each individual class and school community.

The Emotionally Literate School Community

In an Emotionally Literate school each and every person in the school community feels valued and in turn values their colleagues. The school is openly proud of each individual contribution to the whole. Such a school is proud of its diversity and celebrates it. The community is happy in their work and united in a common purpose. Katherine Weare (2004: 106) states that Emotional Literacy is *'at the heart of an efficient and effective school'*. In such a school community all emotions, both comfortable and uncomfortable, are accepted and expressed safely as a normal part of every day. Emotional Literacy is explicit within the school policies and upheld in the values of the school community which promote equity and inclusion through fairness and justice. The staff team has the confidence to be creative and to be supportive of each other.

Final Word

I believe that this research project provides evidence to support the case for Emotional Literacy implementation as an essential curricular element within the taught and wider hidden curriculum in its own right. It requires permeation through the curriculum in our communication, our actions and attitudes, our approaches and behaviour. I have found most children have made significant improvements in self esteem and communication. I observe a greater understanding and tolerance of the needs of others but as Klein (2001) reported, while some children improved, others did not; it is impossible to cure every social problem. What I have found in shifting the

Photo 6.1 Emotional Literacy is a way of being, not just doing. It is an approach to life.

primary focus from attainment targets to building resilience and self esteem, and in giving children the opportunity to develop their communication skills, strategies for emotional control and problem solving, is a method of teaching which is child-centred and builds a creative environment in which it is pleasant to work and learn. I have no concrete evidence that Emotional Literacy raises achievement but we all know that 'feel good, learn good' (Sharp, 2003) is more than a slogan, it is a truism supported by professional practitioner experience.

Further Reading

Bruce, T. (1997) *Early Childhood Education,* 2nd edn. London: Hodder & Stoughton.

Electronic Resources

Go to www.sagepub.co.uk/christinebruce for electronic resources for this chapter:

6.1 Useful Web Addresses

References

Ahn, H.J. (2005) 'Teachers' Discussions of Emotion in Child Care Centers', *Early Childhood Education Journal*, 32 (4): 237–42.

Allan, J. (2003) 'Productive Pedagogies and the Challenge of Inclusion', *British Journal of Special Education*, 30 (4): 175–9.

Altrichter, H., Posch, P. & Somekh, B. (1993) *Teachers Investigate their Work: An Introduction to the Methods of Action Research*. London: Routledge.

Atkin, J., Bastiani, J. & Goode, J. (1988) *Listening to Parents: An Approach to the Improvement of Home–School Relations*. Beckenham, Kent: Croom Helm Ltd.

Austin, R. (2007) *Letting the Outside In: Developing Teaching and Learning Beyond the Early Years Classroom*. Stoke-on-Trent: Trentham Books.

Barlow, J. and Stewart-Brown, S. (2001) 'Understanding Parenting Programmes: Parents' Views', *Primary Health Care Research and Development*, 2: 117–30.

Barnes, J. (2005) '"You could see it on their faces . . .": The Importance of Provoking Smiles in Schools', *Health Education*, 105 (5): 392–400.

Bayley, R. & Broadbent, L. (2001) *Supporting the Development of Listening, Attention and Concentration Skills: Helping Young Children to Listen*. Walsall: Lawrence Educational Publications.

Bell, J. & Opie, C. (2002) *Learning from Research: Getting More from Your Data*. Buckingham: Open University Press.

Bennathan, M. & Boxall, M. (1996) *Effective Interventions in Primary Schools: Nurture Groups*. London: David Fulton Publishers.

Bergen, D. (2002) 'The Role of Pretend Play in Children's Cognitive Development', *Early Childhood Research and Practice*, 4 (1).

Bilton, H. (2002) *Outdoor Play in the Early Years: Management and Innovation*, 2nd edn. London: David Fulton Publishers.

Blakemore, S. & Frith, U. (2005) *The Learning Brain: Lessons for Education*. Oxford: Blackwell Publishing.

British Medical Association (2006) *Child and Adolescent Mental Health: A Guide for Healthcare Professionals*. London: BMA.

Bronfenbrenner, U. (1979) *The Ecology of Human Development: Experiments by Nature and Design*. Cambridge, MA: Harvard University Press.

Brown, J.R. & Dunn, J. (1996) 'Continuities in Emotion Understanding from Three to Six', *Child Development*, 67: 789–802.

Browne, E. (2004) 'Promoting Healthy Schools Through Action Research', *Education 3–13*, 32 (1):14–19.

Bruce, T. (2004) 'Nursery Observation and Assessment'. West Lothian Council In-Service Presentation, 25 October, Ogilvie House, Livingston.

Burton, S. & Shotton, G. (2004) 'Emotional Literacy: Building Emotional Resilience', *Special Children*, September/October: 18–20.

Campbell, A., McNamara, O. & Gilroy, P. (2004) *Practitioner Research and Professional Development in Education*. London: Paul Chapman Publishing.

Carr, D. (2000) 'Emotional Intelligence, PSE and Self Esteem: A Cautionary Note', *Pastoral Care in Education*, 18 (3): 27–33.

Casey, T., Harper, I. & McIntyre, S. (2004) *Inspiring Inclusive Play: The Play Inclusive Action Research Project (P.inc)*. Edinburgh: The Yard.

Cawson, P., Wattam, C., Brooker, S. & Kelly, G. (2000) *Child Maltreatment in the United Kingdom: A Study of the Prevalence of Abuse and Neglect*. NSPCC inform. Available at: www.nspcc.org.uk/inform (accessed 27 November 2009).

Christie, D., Warden, D., Cheyne, B., Fitzpatrick, H. & Reid, K. (1999) 'Assessing and Promoting Children's Social Competence in Schools'. Paper presented at the Scottish Educational Research Association Annual Conference, Dundee, 30 September – 2 October.

Clark, S. (2001) *Unlocking Formative Assessment: Practical Strategies for Enhancing Pupils' Learning in the Primary Classroom*. London: Hodder Murray.

Cohen, L., Manion, L. & Morrison, K. (2000) *Research Methods in Education*, 5th edn. London: RoutledgeFalmer.

Cole, P.M., Martin, S.E. & Dennis, T.A. (2004) 'Emotion Regulation as a Scientific Construct: Methodological Challenges and Directions for Child Development Research', *Child Development*, 75 (2): 317–33.

Collins, M. (2009) *Raising Self-Esteem in Primary Schools: A Whole School Training Programme.* London: SAGE.

Colwell, H. & Hammersley-Fletcher, L. (2004) 'The Emotionally Literate Primary School'. Paper presented at the British Educational Research Association Annual Conference, University of Manchester, 16–18 September.

Cooper, B. (2004) 'Empathy, Interaction and Caring: Teachers' Roles in a Constrained Environment', *Pastoral Care in Education,* 22 (3): 12–21.

Cooper, P. (2008) 'Nurturing Attachment to School: Contemporary Perspectives on Social, Emotional and Behavioural Difficulties', *Pastoral Care in Education*, 26 (1): 13–22.

Cooper, P. & Tiknazy, Y. (2005) 'Progress and Challenge in Nurture Groups: Evidence from Three Case Studies', *British Journal of Special Education*, 32 (4): 211–22.

Cox, T. (2005) 'Pupils' Perspectives on their Education', in K. Topping & S. Maloney (eds), *The RoutledgeFalmer Reader in Inclusive Education.* Oxford: Routledge. pp. 55–72.

Craczyk, P.A., Weissberg, R.P., Payton, J.W., Elias, M.J., Greenberg, M.T. & Zins, J.E. (2000) 'Criteria for Evaluating the Quality of School-Based Social and Emotional Learning Programs', in R. Bar-On & J.D.A. Parker JDA (eds), *The Handbook of Emotional Intelligence. Theory, Developments, Assessment and Application at Home, School and in the Workplace.* San Francisco, CA: Jossey-Bass. pp. 391–410.

Crozier, G. & Reay, D. (2005) *Activating Participation: Parents and Teachers Working Towards Partnership.* Stoke-on-Trent: Trentham Books.

Cutting, A.L. & Dunn (1999) 'Theory of Mind, Emotion Understanding, Language and Family Background: Individual Differences and Inter-relations', *Child Development*, 70 (4): 853–65.

Damasio, A. (2003) *Looking for Spinoza: Joy, Sorrow, and the Feeling Brain.* Orlando: Harcourt Books.

DCELS (2008) *Framework for Children's Learning for 3- to 7-year-olds.* Department for Children, Education, Lifelong Learning and Skills, Welsh Assembly Government Statutory Education Programme. Cardiff: Crown Copyright.

DCSF (2005) *Social & Emotional Aspects of Learning (SEAL) Strategy.* Nottingham: Crown Copyright.

DCSF (2007) *The Children's Plan, Building Brighter Futures.* London: TSO Blackwell.

DCSF (2008) *The Early Years Foundation Stage (EYFS) (Revised).* Nottingham: DCSF. Available at: www.standards.dcsf.gov.uk/eyfs (accessed January 2010).

DCSF (2009) *National Curriculum Values, Aims and Purposes: Values and Purposes Underpinning the School Curriculum.* Available at: http://curriculum.qcda.gov.uk/key-stages-1-and-2/Values-aims-and-purposes/index.aspx (accessed January 2010).

Delamain, C. & Spring, J. (2000) *Developing Baseline Communication Skills.* Bicester: Speechmark Publishing Ltd.

Department of Health and Department for Education & Skills (2004) *Promoting Emotional Health and Wellbeing through the National Healthy Schools Standard.* Nottingham: DfES.

DFES (2004) *Every Child Matters.* London: HMSO.

Donaldson-Feilder, E. & Bond, F. (2004) 'The Relative Importance of Psychological Acceptance and Emotional Intelligence to Workplace Well-Being', *British Journal of Guidance and Counselling,* 32 (2): 187–203.

Dunn, J., Cutting, A.L. & Fisher, N. (2002) 'Old Friends, New Friends: Predictors of Children's Perspective on Their Friends at School', *Child Development,* 73 (2): 625–35.

Durrant, J. & Holden, G. (2006) *Teachers Leading Change: Doing Research for School Improvement.* London: Paul Chapman Publishing.

Dyer, P. (2002) 'A "Box Full of Feelings": Developing Emotional Intelligence in a Nursery Community', in C. Nutbrown (ed.), *Research Studies in Early Childhood Education.* Stoke-on-Trent: Trentham Books. pp. 67–76.

Education (Additional Support for Learning) (Scotland) Act 2004. Available at: www.opsi.gov.uk/legislation/scotland/acts2004/asp_20040004_en_1#pb1 (accessed 13 December 2009).

Elias, M.J., Arnold, H. & Hussey, C.S. (2003) 'EQ, IQ, and Effective Learning and Citizenship', in M.J. Elias, H. Arnold & C.S. Hussey (eds), *EQ+IQ = Best Leadership Practices for Caring and Successful Schools.* Thousand Oaks, CA: SAGE. pp. 3–22.

Elliot, J. (1991) *Action Research for Educational Change.* Buckingham: Open University Press.
Elliot, J. & Sarland, C. (1995) 'A Study of "Teachers as Researchers" in the Context of Award-Bearing Courses and Research Degrees', *British Educational Research Journal,* 21 (3): 371–86.
Evans, J. & Lunt, I. (2002) 'Inclusive Education: Are There Limits?', *European Journal of Special Needs Education,* 17 (1): 1–14.
Farrell, T.S.C. (2004) *Reflective Practice in Action.* London: SAGE.
Faupel, A. (2002) 'Dealing with Anger and Aggression', in P. Gray (ed.), *Working with Emotions.* London: Routledge. pp. 113–26.
Faupel, A. (2003) 'Promoting Emotional Literacy: Its Implications for School and Classroom Practice'. Presentation at the SEBDA (Social Emotional and Behavioural Difficulties Association) International Conference, Communication, Emotion and Behaviour at University of Leicester, 12–14 September. Available at: Nelig.com (accessed 9 October 2004).
Fraser, H., MacDougall, A., Pirrie, A. & Croxford, L. (2001) *Early Intervention in Literacy and Numeracy, Interchange 71.* Edinburgh: SEED.
Frederickson, N. & Cline, T. (2009) *Special Educational Needs, Inclusion and Diversity: A Textbook,* 2nd edn. Buckingham: Open University Press.
Fullan, M. (1991) *The New Meaning of Educational Change.* London: Cassell.
Fullan, M. (1993) *Change Forces: Probing the Depths of Educational Reform.* London: Falmer.
Fullan, M. (2003) *Change Forces: With a Vengeance.* London: Routledge Falmer.
Fullan, M., Hill, P. & Crévola, C. (2006) *Breakthrough.* Thousand Oaks, CA: Corwin Press.
Gardner, H. (1983) *Frames of Mind.* New York: Basic Books.
Gardner, H. (1993) *Multiple Intelligences: The Theory in Practice.* New York: Basic Books.
Garner, P. & Clough, P. (2008) *Father and Son: In and About Education.* Stoke-on-Trent: Trentham Books.
Geddes, H. (2006) *Attachment in the Classroom. The Links between Children's Early Experience, Emotional Well-Being and Performance in School.* London: Worth Publishing.
Geldard, K. & Geldard, D. (1997) *Counselling Children: A Practical Introduction.* London: SAGE.
Gerhardt, S. (2004) *Why Love Matters: How Affection Shapes a Baby's Brain.* London: Routledge.
Glasgow, N.N. & Hicks, C. (2003) *What Successful Teachers Do: Research Based Classroom Strategies for New and Veteran Teachers.* London: SAGE.
Goleman, D. (1996) *Emotional Intelligence: Why it can Matter More than IQ.* London: Bloomsbury Publishing.
Goleman, D. (1998) *Working with Emotional Intelligence.* London: Bloomsbury Publishing.
Gott, J. (2003) 'The School: The Front Line of Mental Health Development?', *Pastoral Care in Education,* 21 (4): 5–13.
Gottman, J. (1997) *The Heart of Parenting.* London: Bloomsburry.
Gray, C. (2002) *My Social Stories Book.* London: Jessica Kingsley Publishers.
Greenfield, S. (2000) *The Private Life of the Brain.* London: Penguin Books.
Grossmann, K.F. (1985) 'The Development of Emotional Expression in a Social Context', in J.T. Spence & C.E. Izard (eds), *Motivation, Emotion, and Personality.* Amsterdam: Elsevier Science Publishers. pp. 305–16.
Haddon, A., Goodman, H., Park, J., & Crick, R.D. (2005) 'Evaluating Emotional Literacy in Schools: The Development of the School Emotional Environment for Learning Survey', *Pastoral Care in Education: An International Journal of Personal, Social and Emotional Development,* 23 (4): 5–16.
Hallam, S., Rhamie, J. & Shaw, J. (2004) *Final Report: Primary Behavior and Attendance Pilot.* London: DfES.
Hamill, P. & Clark, K. (2005) *Additional Support Needs.* Paisley: Hodder Gibson.
Hammond, S. (2007) 'Taking the Inside Out', in R. Austin (ed.), *Letting the Outside In: Developing Teaching and Learning Beyond the Early Years Classroom.* Stoke-on-Trent: Trentham Books. pp. 13–22.
Hanko, G. (2002) 'The Emotional Experience of Teaching: A Priority for Professional Development', in P. Gray (ed.), *Working with Emotions.* London: Routledge. pp. 25–35.
Hargreaves, A. (1992) 'Foreword', in A. Hargreaves & M.G. Fullan (eds), *Understanding Teacher Development.* London: Cassell.
Hargreaves, A. (2000) 'Mixed Emotions: Teachers' Perceptions of Their Interactions with Students!', *Teaching and Teacher Education,* 16: 811–26.
Harris, B. (2007) *Supporting the Emotional Work of School Leaders.* London: SAGE.
Harris, A. & Goodall, J. (2008) 'Do Parents Know they Matter? Engaging all Parents in Learning', *Educational Research,* 50 (3): 277–89.

Hedlund, J. & Sternberg, J. (2000) 'Too Many Intelligences? Integrating Social, Emotional, and Practical Intelligence', in R. Bar-On & J.D.A. Parker (eds), *The Handbook of Emotional Intelligence. Theory, Development, Assessment, and Application at Home, School, and in the Workplace.* San Francisco, CA: Jossey-Bass. pp. 136–67.

Holly, M.L. and Mcloughlin, C.S. (1989) *Perspectives on Teacher Professional Development.* London: Falmer Press.

Humpry, N.P., Curran, A., Morris, E., Farrell, P. & Woods, K. (2007) 'Emotional Intelligence and Education: A Review', *Educational Psychology,* 27: 233–52.

Ironside, V. (1998) *The Huge Bag of Worries.* London: Hodder Children's Books.

Kelly, B., Longbottom, J., Potts, F., Williamson, J. (2004) 'Applying Emotional Intelligence: Exploring the Promoting Alternative and Thinking Strategies Curriculum', *Educational Psychology in Practice,* 20 (3): 221–40.

Klein, R. (2001) 'Never Felt Better', *Times Educational Supplement,* 6 (4).

Knoll, M. & Patti, J. (2003) 'Social-Emotional Learning and Academic Achievement', M.J. Elias, H. Arnold & C.S. Hussey (eds), *EQ+IQ = Best Leadership Practices for Caring and Successful Schools.* Thousand Oaks, CA: SAGE. pp. 36–49.

Kusche, C.A. & Greenberg, M.T. (1994) *The PATHS Curriculum.* Seattle: Developmental Research and Programs. Available at: www.prevention.psu.edu/projects/PATHSPublications.html (accessed 29 December 2009).

Ladd, G.W. & Burgess, K.B. (1999) 'Charting the Relationship Trajectories of Aggressive, Withdrawn, and Aggressive/Withdrawn Children during Early Grade School', *Child Development,* 70 (4): 910–29.

Lawrence, D. (1996) *Enhancing Self Esteem in the Classroom,* 2nd edn. London: Paul Chapman Publishing.

Leavitt, C.H., Tonniges, F. & Rogers, M.F. (2003) 'Good Nutrition – The Imperative for Positive Development', in Marc H. Bornstein, Lucy Davidson, Corey Keyes & Kristin Moore (eds), *Well-Being: Positive Development across the Life Course.* London: Erlbaum. pp. 39–51.

McCarthy, J.R. with Kirkpatrick, S. (2005) 'Negotiating Public and Private: Maternal Mediations of Home–School Boundaries', in G. Crozier & D. Reay (eds), *Activating Participation: Parents and Teachers Working Towards Partnership.* Stoke-on-Trent: Trentham Books. pp. 59–82.

McGinley, S. (2001) 'How Can I Help the Primary School Children I Teach to Develop their Self-Esteem?'. MEd Submission, University of the West of England, Bristol. Available at: www.Jeanmcniff.com (accessed October 2005).

McMinn, J. (2003) 'Speech & Language: Lost for Words', *Special Children,* January: 28–30.

Mathews, G. & Zeidner, M. (2000) 'Emotional Intelligence, Adaptation to Stressful Encounters, and Health Outcomes', in R. Bar-On & J.D.A. Parker (eds), *The Handbook of Emotional Intelligence: Theory, Development, Assessment, and Application at Home, School, and in the Workplace.* San Francisco, CA: Jossey-Bass. pp. 459–89.

Mathews, G., Zeidner, M. & Roberts, R.D. (2002) *Emotional Intelligence: Science and Myth.* Massachusetts: Bradford Books.

Medwell, J., Wray, D., Poulson, L. & Fox, R. (1998) 'Effective Teachers of Literacy', research project commissioned by the Teacher Training Agency (TTA) carried out by the University of Exeter. Available at: www.leeds.ac.uk/educol (accessed 25 January 2006).

Moon, J.A. (1999) *Learning Journals: A Handbook for Academics, Students and Professional Development.* London: Kogan Page.

Morris, E. (2002) *Insight Pre-School: Assessing and Developing Self-Esteem.* London: NFER-Nelson.

Morton, J. (2004) *Understanding Developmental Disorders: A Causal Modelling Approach.* Oxford: Blackwell.

Mosley, J. (1996) *Quality Circle Time.* London: Lucky Duck.

Nutbrown, C. (2006) *Threads of Thinking: Young Children Learning and the Role of Education,* 3rd edn. London: SAGE.

Perry, L., Lennie, C. & Humphrey, N. (2008) 'Emotional Literacy in the Primary Classroom: Teacher Perceptions and Practices ', *Education 3–13,* 36 (1): 27–37.

Pringle, M.K. (1986) *The Needs of Children,* 3rd edn. London: Unwin Hyman.

Pryce, T. (2007) *Circle Time Sessions for Relaxation and Imagination.* London: SAGE.

Roberts, R. (1995) *Self-Esteem and Successful Early Learning.* London: Hodder & Stoughton.

Rogers, B. (2007) *Behaviour Management: A Whole School Approach,* 2nd Edn. London: SAGE.

Rogers, C.R. (1969) *Freedom to Learn.* Columbus, OH: Charles E. Merrill Publishing Company.

Rogers, C.R. & Freiberg, H.J. (1995) *Freedom to Learn,* 3rd edn. New York: Merrill.

Salovey, P. & Mayer, J.D. (1990) 'Emotional Intelligence', *Imagination, Cognition and Personality*, 9: 185–211.

Savage, R. (2001) 'Nurturing Attention and Listening Skills in an Infant School Nurture Group', Southamption Psychology Service. Available at: www.nelig.com (accessed 23 January 2005).

SCCC (Scottish Consultative Council on the Curriculum) (1999). *Curriculum Framework for Children 3–5*. Dundee: The Scottish Office.

Scharfe, E. (2000) 'Development of Emotional Expression, Understanding, and Regulation in Infants and Young Children', in R. Bar-On & J.D.A. Parker (eds), *The Handbook of Emotional Intelligence. Theory, Development, Assessment, and Application at Home, School, and in the Workplace.* San Franciso, CA: Jossey-Bass. pp. 244–62.

Schon, D.A. (1983) *The Reflective Practitioner.* London: Temple Smith.

SEED (2004) *A Curriculum for Excellence: Purposes and Aims.* Available at: Learning & Teaching Scotland website: www.ltscotland.org.uk/curriculumforexcellence/index.asp (accessed 23 November 2009).

SEED (2006) *Parents as Partners in their Children's Learning: Toolkit.* Scottish Executive. Edinburgh.

SEED (2009) *The Curriculum for Excellence: Experiences and Outcomes.* Available at Learning & Teaching Scotland Website: www.ltscotland.org.uk/curriculumforexcellence/responsibilityofall/healthandwellbeing/principlesandpractice/roles and responsibilities.asp

SENDA (2001) The Special Education Needs and Disability Act, 2001, Chapter 10, part 1, section 316. HMSO. Available at: www.opsi.gov.uk/acts/acts2001/20010010.htm (accessed 13 December 2009).

Serbin, L.A., Moskowitz, D.S., Schwartzman, A.E. & Ledingham, J.E. (1991) 'Aggressive, Withdrawn and Aggressive/Withdrawn Children in Adolescence: Into the Next Generation', in J. Pepler & K.H. Rubin (eds), *The Development and Treatment of Childhood Aggression.* Hove and London: LEA Publishers. pp. 55–78.

Shah, M. (2001) *Working with Parents.* Oxford: Heinemann Educational Publishers.

Sharp, P. (2001) *Nurturing Emotional Literacy: Emotionally Literate Schools.* London: David Fulton Publishers.

Sharp, P. (2003) 'Nurturing Emotional Literacy'. Presentation at the Osiris Educational Emotional Literacy Conference, 26 March, London.

Sheppy, S. (2009) *Personal, Social and Emotional Development in the Early Years Foundation Stage.* London: David Fulton Publishers.

Silveira, W.R., Trafford, G. & Musgrove, R. (1988) *Children Need Groups. A Practical Manual for Group Work with Young Children.* Aberdeen: Aberdeen University Press.

Simpson, L.J. (2001) *Into the Garden of Dreams: Pathways to Imagination for 5–8s: A Relaxing Resource for Teachers to Help Raise Children's Self-esteem and Expression in the Classroom.* Dunstable: Brilliant Publications.

Smith, A. (2004) *The Brain's Behind It: New Knowledge About the Brain and Learning.* Stafford: Network Educational Press.

Smith, C. (2003) 'Don't Get Emotional About Intelligence', *Times Educational Supplement*, 12 (9).

Somekh, B. (1995) 'The Contribution of Action Research to Development in Social Endeavours: A Position Paper on Action Research Methodology', *British Educational Research Journal*, 21 (3): 339–55.

Stenhouse, L. (1975) *An Introduction to Curriculum Research and Development.* London: Heinemann.

Todd, L. (2007) *Partnerships for Inclusive Education: A Critical Approach to Collaborative Working.* London: RoutledgeFalmer.

Topping, K. & Homes, E.A. (1998) 'Promoting Social Competence'. Available at: www.dundee.ac.uk/fedsoc/research/projects/socialcompetence (accessed July 2005).

Topping, K. & Maloney, S. (eds) (2005) *The RoutledgeFalmer Reader in Inclusive Education.* Oxford: Routledge.

Topping, K., Holmes, E.A. & Bremner, W. (2000) 'The Effectiveness of School-Based Programmes for the Promotion of Social Competence', in R. Bar-On & J.D.A. Parker (eds), *The Handbook of Emotional Intelligence: Theory, Development, Assessment, and Application at Home, School, and in the Workplace.* San Francisco, CA: Jossey-Bass. p. 411–32.

Tripp, D. (1993) *Critical Incidents in Teaching: Developing Professional Judgement.* London: Routledge.

Vygotsky, L.S. (1978) *Mind in Society: The Development of Higher Psychological Processes.* Cambridge: Harvard University Press.

Walden, T.A. & Field, T.M. (1982) 'Discrimination of Facial Expressions by Preschool Children', *Child Development,* 53 (5): 1312–19.

Walford, G. (2001) *Doing Qualitative Educational Research: A Personal Guide to the Research Process*. London: Routledge.
Walker, B.M. & MacLure, M. (2005) 'Home School Partnerships in Practice', in G. Crozier & D. Reay (eds), *Activating Participation: Parents and Teachers Working Towards Partnership*. Stoke-on-Trent: Trentham Books. pp. 97–110.
Weare, K. (2004) *Developing the Emotionally Literate School*. London: Paul Chapman.
Weare K. (2007) 'Delivering Every Child Matters: The Central Role of Social and Emotional Learning in Schools', *Education 3–13*, 35 (3): 239–48.
Weare, K. & Gray, G. (2002) *What Works in Developing Children's Emotional and Social Competence and Wellbeing?* Nottingham: DfES.
Whitehead, J. (1989) 'Creating a Living Educational Theory from Questions of the Kind, "How Do I Improve my Practice?"', *Cambridge Journal of Education*, 19 (1): 41–52.
Whitehead, J. (2007) 'Telling It Like It Is: Developing Social Stories for Children in Mainstream Primary Schools', *Pastoral Care in Education*, 25 (4): 35–41.
Wrigley, T. (2005) 'The Policy of Improvement: What Hope Now for Working Class Kids?', in P. Clarke (ed.), *Improving Schools in Difficulty*. London: Continuum. pp. 22–42.
Zeidner, M., Roberts, R.D. & Mathews, G. (2002) 'Can Emotional Intelligence be Schooled? A Critical Review', *Education Psychologist*, 37: 215–31.
Zins, J.E., Weissberg, R.P., Wang, M.C. & Walberg, H. (2004) *Building Academic Success on Social and Emotional Learning*. New York: Columbia University Teachers College.

Index

The abbreviation 'E.L.' in subheadings indicates 'Emotional Literacy'; page numbers in *italics* indicate figures; page numbers in **bold** indicate photos

achievement, rewarding 33
action research
  Altrichter model 46
  appropriateness for project 11, 88
  impact on reflectiveness 90, 91
action research project
  baseline for action research 9–10
  definition of E.L. 6
  description 2–3
  effectiveness 87–9
  refined through reflection on findings 13
  research question 9
aggressive play *64*, 65
  see also rowdy play
Ahn, H.J. 51
Allan, J. 33
Altrichter, H. 9, 46
anger, discussion **58**, 59, *86*
Atkin, J. 72
attachment, and resilience 77
Austin, R. 70

babies, use of soft toys 36
Barlow, J. 53
Barnes, J. 44
Baseline Communication and Language 35, 36
baseline measurements, 9–10, 25
Bayley, R. 9, 35
behaviour,
  taking responsibility for 23
  see also challenging behaviour; positive behaviour
behavioural problems 25–6, *90*
Bell, J. 90
benefits of Emotional Literacy 6, 8
Bennathan, M. 24
Bergen, D. 51
Bilton, H. 65
body language, observations 89
boisterous play *see* rowdy play
Bond, F. 7
boundaries 44
Boxall, M. 24
brain, role in emotion 3, 23–4
break, involvement of parents 73–4
British Medical Association 77
Broadbent, L. 9, 35
Bronfenbrenner model 5
Brown, J.R. 5, 53, 68

Campbell, A. 10, 90
Cawson, P. 22
CBeebies Emotion Theatre 55
challenging behaviour 35–6, *90*
  see also discipline
child-centred learning environment 16, 17, 22
chill time 16–17, 33
Christie, D. 4, 6
circle time
  parachute activities **62**, 64
  procedures 46–7
  small groups 38
Clark, K. 29, 38
class contracts 22–3
classrooms
  ambience for meetings 72
  appearance 32
  arrangement to support E.L. 16
  entrances 20
Cline, T. 44, 68
Clough, P. 74
coffee meetings, for parents 69
Cohen, L. 3, 10
collaborative working
  staff 77–8, 88
  see also partnerships
colours, use to express feelings *20*
Colwell, H. 44, 92
communication
  with parents 68–72
  see also relationships
communication skills, developing 24–5, 25–6, 47–8, *64*, 65, 85
Community puzzle bags 20
contracts, class 22–3
Cooper, B. 24, 30, 31, 77, 78
cooperative play 50, 64, 65, 66
curriculum, importance of E.L. 8–9, 20–1, 30
Cutting, A.L. 85

Damasio, A. 24
data collection
  from pupils and parents 9–10, 12–13, 82–7, *82*, *83*, *84*, *85*, *86*, *87*
  see also observation; reflective journals
DCELS 8
DCSF 4, 8, 9, 32, 33, 44, 70, 71
Delamain, C. 25, 36, 47, 48, 92
Developing Baseline Communication Skills 47, 48, 93
DfES 30
discipline 23
displays **19**, **53**, **56**, **57**, **58**, **79**, **80**
Donaldson-Feilder, E. 7
drama, guided play 49–52
dressing up boxes 52
Dunn, J. 5, 53, 68, 85
Durrant, J. 70
Dyer, P. 24

Early Years Framework (EYF)
  principles 32, 33, 44
  recognition of E.L. 30

education, importance of E.L. 7–8
Elias, M.J. 6, 30
Elliott, J. 11
Emergency bags 20
emotional abuse, of children 22
Emotional Intelligence 3–4, *4*
Emotional Literacy
  continuum of development 5, *5*
  description 1–2, 3, 81
  learning spaces for 17, **19**
  research on effects in schools 7
emotional vocabulary interviews and questionnaires
  pre-research 10, 11, 12–13, *12*, *13*
  post-research 83–5, *85*, *86*, 88
emotions
  effect on learning 23–4
  recognition from facial expression 85, *86*
  see also feelings
empathy
  goal of E.L. 5
  towards children 67–8
empowerment, pupils 24, 38
Evans, J. 44
exclusion from school 30
extension activities **3**, 55–60, **55–61**, 63, **63**

facial expressions, perception 85, *86*
Farrell, T.S.C. 26
fathers, involvement 74
Faupel, A. 7, 8, 18, 31, 44
feelings
  expression 10, *12*, *20*, 37, 39, 49, *49*
  graffiti activity 58, 59
  use of photos 52, 54
  use of stories 48, 55
  see also emotions
Field, T.M. 85
focus groups *see* small groups
Foundation Stage Framework, recognition of E.L. 30
Frederickson, N. 44, 68
friendship activity **59**, 60
Fullan, M. 9, 77, 79, 90, 91

Gardner, H. 4, 8
Garner, P. 74
Geddes, H. 77
Gerhardt, S. 21
Glasgow, N.N. 71
Goleman, D. 3, 5, 6, 24
Goodall, J. 70
Gottman, J. 76
graffiti activity **58**, 59
Gray, G. 7, 37
Greenberg, M.T. 39
Greenfield, S. 19
Grossmann, K.F. 22

Haddon, A. 88
Hamill, P. 29, 38
Hammersley-Fletcher, L. 44, 92

Hammond, S. 19, 22, 73
Hanko, G. 76
Hargreaves, A. 8, 11, 75, 76
Harris, A. 70
Harris, B. 75, 77
Hicks, C. 71
hierarchy of needs 2
holism, in E.L. 24
Holly, M.L. 11
home-school relationships 68–72
home-time 20
Homes, E.A. 7
homework 70–1

imaginative play 48–52
inclusion, in education 29–30
instant fun activities 23
interviews, pupils 10, *12*, 82–3, *82*, *83*, 88

key worker system 47–8
Klein, R. 26, 93
Knoll, M. 6
Kusche, C.A. 39

language use, by adults 23
learning environment
  for E.L. 16–20
  sounds and smells 33, 37
  supportiveness 2, 32
lighting 32
listening to children 7, 22, 24, 32, 37, 44, 74, 90
Lunt, I. 44

McCarthy, J.R. 71
McGinley, S. 25, 90
Mcloughlin, C.S. 11
Maclure, M. 70–1, 72
Maslow, A. 2
Mathews, G. 5, 7
Mayer, J.D. 1–2, 3
micro-environments 5
minimalist resources 51–2, **51**
Moon, J.A. 90
Morris, E. 44
Morton, J. 77
Mosley, J. 48
multiple intelligences 4
music, to create mood 32, 37, 59

newsletters and bulletins 69
noise, learning to respond to 16–17
non-verbal communication skills 25–6
number scale, to express feelings *20*, 49, *49*
nursery practice
  communication skills development 47–8
  observations 26, 88–9
  parachute activities **61–2**, 63
  use of photography 52–3, **53**
  pupil interviews 10, *12*, 83, *83*

nursery practice *cont.*
use of puppets 38–40
use of small groups 35–6
use of story and drama 49–50
nurture group approach 24, 48

observations
for reflective practice 26, 88–9
for research data 86
see also reflective journals
older children
assisting with transitions 74
use of puppets 40–2
use of story and drama 52, 55
open evenings 69
Opie, C. 90
outdoor play *64*, 65–6, **65**
parachute activities **62**, 64
ownership, class space 16

Paper Chain People activity 55, **57**
parachute activities **61–2**, 63–4
parent meetings 69, 71–2
parents
background information on child 22, 69
child's relationship with 22
communication with 68–72
emotional vocabulary questionnaires 10, 11, 12–13, 83–5, *85*, *86*, 88
influence on educational achievement 68
involvement in school activities 73–4
workshops for 69, 73
partnerships
with other professionals 69, 76
with parents 68-9, 70–2
see also collaborative working
Patti, J. 6
peace and serenity activity **58**, 59
pedagogy, implications of E.L. 92–3
person-centred ideals 15
personal space *40*, 66
photos, use 20, 41, 52–5
pictorial timetables 32, **34**
play *see* imaginative play; outdoor play
playtime, parental involvement 73–4
positive attitude, towards children 67
positive behaviour, promoting 33, **34**
pretend play 48–52
primary practice
communications skills development 48
outdoor activities 65–6
use of photos 53–5
pupil interviews 10, 82, *82*
use of puppets 40–3, **41**, **42–3**, **60**
use of small groups 36–8
use of story and drama 51–2
Pringle, M.K. 2
professional practice, implications of E.L. project 92–3
Promoting Alternative Thinking Strategies (PATHS), use of puppets 39–40
pupil empowerment 24, 38

puppet buddies 38–43, **41**, **42–3**, **60**
puppet families 41–2
puppets 38–43, **41**, **42–3**, **60**
  use in interviews 10

quality learning 23
questionnaires, for parents 10, 11, 12–13, *13*, 22, 83–5, *85*, *86*, 88
quiet activities 17
quiet spaces 17, **18**

reflection
  advantages 89–91
  by teachers 36
  during research 11
  spaces for children 17, **18**
reflection in action 88
reflective journal extracts *27*, *49*
  behavioural problems *87*, *90*
  discussion of emotion *86*
  feelings *37*, *54*
  key workers 48
  outdoor play *64*
  parachute play *62*, *63*
  quiet children *49*
  use of puppets *39*, *40*
reflective journals 11, 26
relationships
  assisting children with 22
  friendship activity **59**, 60
  home-school 68–72
  staff 69, 76
  teacher-pupil 33
research on Emotional Literacy 7
research project *see* project
resilience 23
  and attachment 77
  developing through drama 50
  and self esteem 31, 44
  through use of puppets 39–40
resources
  minimalist 51–2, **51**
  organisation 32
  provided by parents 74
responsibility, pupils 16, 23
Roberts, R. 77, 90
Rogers, C.R. 7–8, 18, 24, 65
rowdy play *64*
  parachute activities **62**, 64–5
  structuring 48–9
rules
  for circle time 47
  creation 32
  for outdoor play 66

safe environments 32–3
Salovey, P. 1–2, 3
Sarland, C. 11
Savage, R. 24
SCCC 3

scent, use of 32, 37
Scharfe, E. 85
Schon, D.A. 88
school community, effect of E.L. 92, 93
Scotland, curriculum and E.L. 7, 8, 30
SEED 8
self awareness 31
self esteem
  and resilience 31, 44
  teachers 76–7
self image 43–4
semi-structured interviews, pupils 10, *12*, 82–3, *82*, *83*
SENDA 30
sense of belonging
  establishment 15, 21, 31
  through key groups 48
Serbin, L.A. 68
serenity activity **58**, 59
Shah, M. 70, 74
Sharp, P. 4, 18, 76
Sheppy, S. 60
shy children 25, *25*, 36
Silveira, W.R. 35
small groups
  based on social skills 35–6
  circle time 38
  parachute activities 63
  for quiet children 36, 48
  teaching 15
  withdrawal from main class 24
small world play 52
social skills, support for development 35–8
social story pictures 35
Somekh, B. 11, 91
spaces
  for E.L. activities 17–20
  for parents 68
special person chart 17
Spring, J. 25, 36, 47, 48, 92
staff *see* support staff; teachers
start of school day, welcoming parents 68
starting school, adaptation to 12
Stenhouse, L. 91
Stewart-Brown, S. 53
stories, use of drama 49–52
success of E.L. *86*, 87, *87*, 92
support staff 72–3

teachers
  as attachment figures 44, 77
  classroom space 18–19, **21**
  use of emotional literacy 74–5
  empathy 67–8
  involvement in project 91
  mutual support 76
  partnerships with other professionals 69, 76
  self esteem 76–7
teachers' desks 18–19, **21**
teaching assistants 72–3

teaching and learning
  effect of E.L. on quality 23
  philosophy 15
  process for enhancing E.L. 24
teaching space 20
team building activities 50, 64, 65, 66
thinking spaces 17, **18**
Three Billy Goats Gruff, The, use of story 49–50, **50–1**
tidy-up time 20
Tiknazy, Y. 24
timetables
  importance of flexibility 31
  pictorial 32, **34**
Todd, L. 30, 70, 78
toddlers, use of soft toys 36
Topping, K. 7
toy animals
  use 35–6
  see also puppets
transitions
  help from older children 74
  meetings for parents 69
  use of photos 52
  use of puppets 40
triangulation methods 9–10, 48

United Kingdom
  E.L. in the curriculum 9
  see also Scotland; Wales

very young children, use of toy animals 36
video recording, observations 89
visualisation activity 57–9
Vygotsky, L.S. 85

Walden, T.A. 85
Wales, curriculum and E.L. 7, 8
Walford, G. 86, 89, 90
Walker, B.M. 70–1, 72
wall of fame 17
WALT learning goals 38
Weare, K. 4, 7, 37, 79, 93
Whitehead, J. 90
whole class approach 48
whole-school approach 78–80
WILF criteria 38
withdrawal from class, small groups 24
withdrawn (quiet) children 25, *25*, 36
workplace, benefits of E.L. 6
workshops for parents 69, 73
Worry Beads activity 55
worry box 33
Wrigley, T. 31

Zeidner, M. 7

OUTDOOR PROVISION IN THE EARLY YEARS

Edited by **Jan White**

Outdoor education offers children special contexts for play and exploration, real experiences and contact with the natural world and the community. To help ensure young children thrive and develop in your care, this book provides essential information on how to make learning outdoors a rich and valuable part of their daily life.

Written by a team of experts in the field, this book focuses on the core values of effective outdoor provision, and is packed with ideas to try out in practice. Topics covered include:

- the role of play in learning outdoors
- meaningful experiences for children outdoors
- the role of the adult outdoors
- creating a dynamic and flexible outdoor environment
- dealing with challenge, risk and safety
- including every child in outdoor learning.

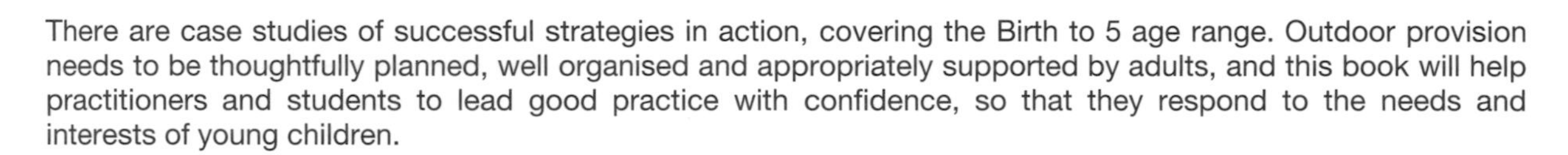

There are case studies of successful strategies in action, covering the Birth to 5 age range. Outdoor provision needs to be thoughtfully planned, well organised and appropriately supported by adults, and this book will help practitioners and students to lead good practice with confidence, so that they respond to the needs and interests of young children.

CONTENTS

Jan White Introduction / **Felicity Thomas and Stephanie Harding** The role of play: Play outdoors as the medium and mechanism for well-being, learning and development / **Liz Magraw** Following children's interests: Child-led experiences that are meaningful and worthwhile / **Tim Waller** Adults are essential: The roles of adults outdoors / **Jan White** Capturing the difference: The special nature of the outdoors / **Ros Garrick** A responsive environment: Creating a dynamic, versatile and flexible environment / **Claire Warden** Offering rich experiences: Contexts for play, exploration and talk / **Di Chilvers** As long as they need: The vital role of time / **Helen Tovey** Achieving the balance: Challenge, risk and safety / **Theresa Casey** Outdoor play for everyone: Meeting the needs of individuals / **Miranda Murray** Taking an active part: Everyday participation and effective consultation / After Word: Learning through Landscapes

March 2011 · 160 pages
Cloth (978-1-4129-2308-8) / Paper (978-1-4129-2309-5)